ABCs
of
Activity Based Management

ABCs
of
Activity Based Management

✦

Crushing Competition Through
Performance Improvement

William Frost

iUniverse, Inc.
New York Lincoln Shanghai

ABCs of Activity Based Management
Crushing Competition Through Performance Improvement

Copyright © 2005 by William Frost

iUniverse books may be ordered through booksellers or by contacting:

iUniverse
2021 Pine Lake Road, Suite 100
Lincoln, NE 68512
www.iuniverse.com
1-800-Authors (1-800-288-4677)

ISBN-13: 978-0-595-35871-7 (pbk)
ISBN-13: 978-0-595-80328-6 (ebk)
ISBN-10: 0-595-35871-3 (pbk)
ISBN-10: 0-595-80328-8 (ebk)

Printed in the United States of America

Contents

Introduction

We have entered a period of unparalleled competition in the services industry. Deregulation, privatization of foreign firms, and the increasing global economy has created a very volatile environment. Banks, airlines, insurance agencies, and others are seeking to be the best and crush their competition. But there is only room for one at the top. Will it be you and your company? Or will you be the one that gets trampled on and passed by. Will you rise to the challenge? Or will you continue to wallow in the same old drudgery that your company has been doing for years?

There are countless books that claim to tell you how to compete and win in these environments. You've probably read many of them. The books talk about the power of Activity Based Costing/Management (ABC/ABM), continuous improvement, *etc*. The authors even define them and tell you it's the best thing since sliced bread. They promise how much you'll improve the bottom line, yet you still struggle to implement their ideas. Your company continues to stumble along with mediocre profitability, reporting, and process improvement. And honestly, how much has your company's profitability improved after all that? Lets face it…if you want to win, it is time to make a stand and TAKE ACTION!

If you want a book on theory, philosophies, and generalities then read something else. But if you want to succeed in business and crush your competition, this is the book for you. ABCs of Activity Based Management is different. It spends very little time on the philosophies and warm and gushy stuff. The purpose of this book is to provide practical guidance on implementing and utilizing Activity Based Management to improve your organization.

Many companies struggle with ABM and process improvement. There is a lot of hard work and creativity required to get it to work. On many occasions, people learn from the school of hard knocks before coming up with a true improvement-oriented system. These lessons are unnecessary. Imagine having a resource containing all that information and experience at your fingertips. The ABCs of Activity Based Management is that resource. It fills the voids that other books and programs left behind.

Many of the examples used in this book are illustrated using a fictional company aptly named Average Business Incorporated (ABI). This fictional company is a small community bank that aspires to become better than it is. It desires to become better than average or even best of breed (BOBI) by getting a handle on what drives the company's profitability and how to prioritize areas for improvement. Activity Based Management (ABM) will help them to achieve this goal.

ABM development is a straightforward step-by-step process. It is a matter of understanding what you want to accomplish in the end, then working backwards to find the best way to do it. From that stand point the first few sections will cover why this information is useful, who uses it and how to strategize some goals to improve your organization. This will form the basis of what you want your ABM system to be and do. Then we'll walk step by step through finding activity times, calculating ABC costs, and designing ABM to get the most out of it. Finally, the book will cover how to utilize the information for managing your operations and process improvement.

In the Take Action section, we'll discuss several process improvement topics including: Benchmarking, Theory of Constraints, Capacity Management, and Budgeting/Planning. With this book, you will learn what to do, how to do it, why to do it, and what pitfalls to avoid. The steps presented here are proven to be among the best in the services industry. Some of the ideas in this book may be controversial in your organization. So, keep an open mind and keep your eye on the ball.

The ABCs of Activity Based Management is an insightful book and a valuable resource for those implementing new ABM systems, as well as for ABM practitioners who already use or profess to use ABM. Many people will read this book and recognize dozens of similarities with their own organizations. ABCs of Activity Based Management is the culmination of many certifications and degrees (including a BS in Industrial Engineering and a Master of Business Administration), as well as over a decade of practical experience in both manufacturing and the financial services industries. I encourage you to leverage this knowledge and experience by using this book as a cookie cutter. Copy the techniques presented here to create and fine-tune your own ABM system. Only then can you propel your organization forward through ABM and continuous process improvement.

Background: Importance of Costing Information

Good costing information is vital to a corporation's survival. Looking at the bottom line tells a company how profitable it is, but yields no information on how to improve. Process improvement systems based on ABM provide this kind of information and help managers to run the business as efficiently as possible. From the Chief Executive Officer (CEO) down to the average employee, every group and individual of the company has a reason or need for solid, accurate, and reliable costing information. This book will show how to design a system to provide this type of information.

When designing a system it is important to understand who will utilize the information and what their interests are. This understanding provides focus for developing reports and making the information as useable as possible. The section below shows a few of the users of ABM information and their vantage points.

Users of ABM and Process Improvement Information

Senior Leaders (CEO, CFO and other executives)

Senior leaders and executives monitor profitability very closely. A key part of profitability is the organizational costs and the utilization of the organization's resources. They base their decisions on facts and intuition. A good ABM system provides executives with such facts as: operational efficiency, profitability by Product Line and Business Unit, and most importantly, the efficiency and profitability trends.

Based on this type of information Senior Leaders probe further. They will ask such questions as: Is profitability increasing or decreasing? And is productivity increasing or decreasing? *etc.* These are important things to know. The answers tell executives how the company is performing. They tell which areas are doing well, and are reflected in the corporation's metrics (ROA, ROE, *etc.*). Trends, combined with the executive's own industry knowledge and experience, help leaders make better decisions to enhance and guide the future of the company.

Product Managers

Product Managers want to know if their Products are profitable. Their incentives are often based on the sales generated and the profits reaped from their Products. Understanding the processes and the resources that the processes utilize, helps Product Managers make better decisions. Better decisions improve the Product's profitability and aid in successful launches of future Products. Product Managers are keenly aware that to improve the profitability of their Products they only have two choices:

1.   To increase revenues (increase fees, Unit Prices, *etc.*), or

2.   To decrease costs through Activity Based Management.

Increasing fees and Unit Prices will work in the short term. But continuous or sudden increases will alienate the customer base and cause the company to become less competitive.

In contrast, reducing costs through process improvement increases the profitability and the company's competitiveness. Product Managers want to know what makes up the cost and what affects increasing volume or demand will have on the processes (costs). Knowing the make up of the costs and the capacity of the processes, Product Managers can make informed decisions about a Product and more accurately estimate the profitability of future Products. Process Knowledge also helps the Product Manager guide and prioritize process improvement efforts.

Finally, Product Managers are also concerned with trends. How is the Product doing? Is the profitability increasing or decreasing? Is the demand increasing or decreasing? Are the processes becoming more efficient or less? Are customers switching from one Product to another, what's the trend? Just like the executives, combining solid information with a good knowledge of the industry, allows Product Managers to make better decisions.

Sales and Relationship Executives

Closely related to the Product Managers are the Sales and Relationship Executives. These executives are responsible for customer profitability. They want to know if their customers are profitable. Their incentives and bonuses hinge on the profitability information. So, they want to maximize customer profitability for both their benefit and that of the corporation. In this sense, what is good for the individual is also best for the shareholder. Therefore, it is crucial that the costs assigned to the customer and Products for profitability reporting are appropriate and include all aspects of the corporation. (Notice I am careful not to use the word full-absorption here. We'll cover that later in this book.)

Sales Executives, like Product Managers, have two choices for improving profitability: increasing revenues or decreasing costs. They also have the same two effects: increasing competitiveness or decreasing competitiveness. Again, creative solutions can be found to increase revenues, but the corporation has no control over how many fees and service charges a customer is willing to accept.

In contrast, the company has a great deal of control over how to improve processes. The company also has control over evaluating its customers and their profitability to know which ones are the most profitable. Often, the majority of customers are unprofitable or barely profitable. In fact, the top 20% of the customers often drive the company's overall profitability. Imagine how a little analysis on the bottom 80% could help turn around the unprofitable ones and increase profits from those that are just barely profitable. Sales Executives can work with marketing to analyze the characteristics of their most profitable customers, identify other customers or potential customers with the same characteristics and then focus their "new sale" efforts on these customers. A good ABM and profitability system provides the data to analyze these situations and track the results of any actions that are taken.

Organizational Leaders

Department and profit center managers have the greatest control and opportunity to improve the processes from the inside. They have the influence to make on-going, immediate improvements that can reap rewards each and every time a function is performed. They lead groups of employees who perform the day-to-day servicing of the customer. Organizational Leaders know what the day-to-day problems and aggravations are. These aggravations act as speed bumps in the servicing of customers and waste valuable resources. If the problems can be eliminated, chances are very good that the improvements will enhance the bottom line. Good managers know this. Great leaders are passionate about this and ACT ON IT!

Unfortunately, some companies try to hold these managers responsible for Product or customer profitability. This is attempted by allocating expenses and revenues to the department. This allocation provides little use for process or financial improvement. It is very difficult to improve things you have no control over. As a result, these types of situations lead to an "Us and Them" mentality. You spend more time arguing over the allocation methodology than improving the processes. This will be discussed in more detail later.

Finance and Accounting

The Finance and Accounting departments typically take care of the financial statements and maintain the General Ledger system used as a basis for the financial statements. They focus on total company profitability or Profit/Loss by Business Unit. Poor profitability often leads to a tendency to cut costs and trim down the organization. Of course, this should be done only when necessary. The Finance and Accounting groups provide details to Senior Executives who make the final decision on such cuts. To do this, they need the best, most accurate cost information possible. If a decision has to be made, it is better base it on good information than on bad data or "hunches".

Purchasing and Facility Managers

Purchasing and Facilities Managers are often involved in process improvement initiatives to decrease overhead, materials, outside services, and occupancy costs. Facility Managers also look to minimize the unused occupancy space while still leaving room for future growth. It's a delicate balancing act between having too much and having too little unused space. Again, a good ABM system provides tools for managers to monitor these situations with increased insight.

Activity Based Management Teams

Activity Based Management Teams are the last, but most obvious, group to utilize the Activity Based Management information. These teams may also be called: Cost Accounting, Process Improvement Team, Industrial Engineering, *etc.* ABM Teams rely on ABC costs, activity times and time study documentation to prioritize, analyze, report on and improve processes. They may also utilize existing ABM data to predict the cost of future Products or services. Process improvement is something that is best done in-house so that all the knowledge and experience gained through the project remains within the organization. This pool of expertise can then be drawn upon to improve other areas.

Companies often hire outside consultants to come in and recommend improvements. Consultants can be a wonderful source of information on how others are using ABM and improving processes. They provide knowledge and insight from many organizations and can be used as a benchmarking resource.

However, the actual expertise for improvement must be developed and maintained in house. Consultants can spark many great ideas, but the boots on the ground do the real work. Remember, money is not saved when the consultant receives his payment and leaves. Evaluating and implementing the ideas is the real challenge. Financials improve only when headcount is reduced, excess resources are sold/disposed of, transaction volume is increased, process improvements are made that will last 2+ years, customer's receive better service for a lesser price, *etc.* You get the picture. The benefits of Activity Based Management and process improvement are only realized when the improvements are implemented.

Costing Systems

There are four different systems of cost development: Average Costing, Full Absorption Costing, Lifecycle Costing, and Activity Based Costing. There is much literature about the pitfalls and benefits of each of these, so we won't spend much time on it here. This is a how-to and trouble-shooting book on ABM, not a book on costing philosophies. But, we will briefly review each one below for background purposes.

AVERAGE COSTING

Average Costing is by far the easiest and fastest calculation to make. You simply take the total expenses and divide by the total volume to get the average cost. This technique works great for one time quick analysis and for generating a "rule of thumb". For example, on average it costs $1.75 per transaction.

Over the long haul, the results can be misleading. The average transaction cost is volume based and fluctuates in tandem with volume fluctuations. If you calculate an average cost on a regular basis then your transaction costs fluctuate every period. Consequently, Sales folks will have a difficult time quoting a price for the service since the cost is constantly moving. For example:

Table 1.1

	Period 1	Period 2
Dept. Expenses	$25,000	$24,500
Dept. Volume	15,000	12,000
Average Cost	$1.67	$2.04

Transaction costs are used for profitability reporting and pricing. Unfortunately, Average Costing is like trying to hit a moving target. At one time Sales folks price the service to be profitable based on a cost of $1.67. Then when the volume drops to 12,000 the average transaction cost increases to $2.04. Now,

1

suddenly their services and customers appear under water. Thus, Average Costing is great for a quick ad-hoc analysis and generating quick rules of thumb, but it is generally not used as a long-term approach for profitability.

FULL ABSORPTION COSTING

Full Absorption Costing fully absorbs/includes all the expenses incurred by Products and services into the total volume. Full Absorption is a more detailed and robust way of doing Average Costing. You can use actual historical volumes or forecast/budgeted volumes depending on what result you want. Unfortunately, this method assumes the resources are fully utilized by the given volume with no unused capacity.

The main benefit of Full Absorption is that all your costs are included in the transaction cost that the sales team uses for pricing. But, it also inflates the true transaction cost per item since your costs include the cost of idle capacity. An inflated cost causes the sales folks to quote a higher (less competitive) price. In fact, you may be pricing yourself out of the market.

Full Absorption and Average Costing can become downward spirals. As the price increases due to full absorption, you get less sales volume. As you get less volume, the transaction cost increases (same expenses divided by a now smaller volume) to ensure full absorption. This cost increase causes the sales team to increase the price to cover the new fully absorbed cost, which results in even lower volumes. The cycle continues until you have priced yourself out of the market. Full Absorption is good for quick ad-hoc analyses, but it is usually not used for long term costing, profitability and process improvement initiatives.

LIFE CYCLE COSTING (LCC)

Life Cycle Costing is the process of developing the flow of a transaction through the entire corporation to determine the cost. This technique is best visualized using a flow chart like the one shown in Figure 1.1.

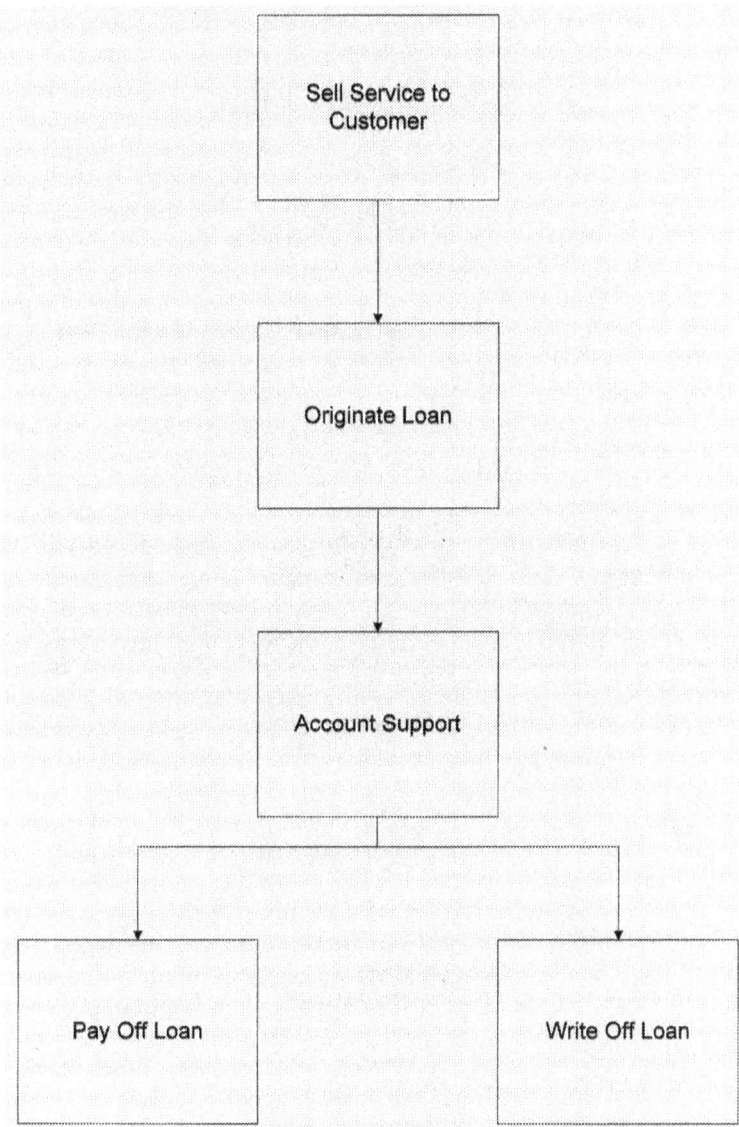

Figure 1.1

Life Cycle Costing is a great way to come up with a rough cost of providing a service and can be quickly developed by a cross functional team of folks knowledgeable with the process. Some of the boxes above, such as Account Support and Pay-Off a Loan can be broken down into more detail.

Account Support	• Update Account information
	• Update Interest Rates and fees
	• Initiate a Payment
	• Maintain a Delinquent Loan
Pay-Off a Loan	• Process final payment
	• Process Title (if applicable) and mail to customer

The main benefit of Life Cycle Costing is that it is very visually oriented. The flow charts are very easy to develop and explain. Life Cycle charts are also good inputs to a swim lane analysis, which can determine unnecessary hand-offs and spark process improvement ideas.

The drawback is that it is very difficult to put this type of cost into a system and use it for management and decision-making. The reason is that the flow chart reflects the combined effort of many departments. Many departments work on multiple Products and Cost Drivers. So, each box above may only represent a portion of that department's workflow. The remainder of the department's work is likely spread across other LCC flows. Further, Managers typically manage a whole department not a part of a department. So developing one Life Cycle isn't good enough. You would only be accounting for that portion of the department's costs that was included in the Life Cycle. Realistically, you would need to develop many of these flow charts and link them all together in a system before you could account for the entire department's costs. This method becomes a very tiresome, grueling process and you never seem to finish enough to use for management reporting. Thus, Life Cycle Costing is not an effective means for on-going costing and management. Life Cycle Charts are important and later we'll see how they can be immensely useful in developing ABC.

ACTIVITY BASED COSTING/MANAGEMENT

Activity Based Costing/Management is the most robust and useful costing system in use today. The concept of Activity Based Costing is fairly simple and easy to understand. The basic steps in Activity Based Costing are outlined below.

Steps in Developing ABC/M

1. Strategy and Planning

2. Finding Resources

3. Define Products and Cost Drivers

4. Select Department or Area to Study

5. Calculate Activity Times

6. Calculate ABC Costs

7. Summarize/Roll-Up Costs

8. Take Action!

ABC VERSUS ABM

So, what is Activity Based Management and how does it differ from Activity Based Costing?

Activity Based Costing (ABC)

Activity Based Costing is the process of designing and developing transaction costs for the services and Products provided by a business. ABC includes analyzing your business to determine what customer actions drive the costs (often referred to Cost Drivers), and performing cost studies to determine the costs related to the drivers. ABC costs are most often used for Product and customer profitability reporting as part of ABM.

Activity Based Management (ABM)

Activity Based Management (ABM) is the art of utilizing the Activity Based Costs to provide leaders with quantifiable guidance on the management of the company's resources. Activity Based Costs tell you what it should cost to provide a service. ABM takes it one step further. In ABM you compare your calculated ABC costs to the actual expenses incurred during a given time period. This comparison tells you how well you are managing your resources. ABC tells you what the costs are; ABM shows you how to improve.

The word "art" was specifically chosen to describe ABM since it is not an exact science. Decisions made by management are rarely black and white. Instead, ABM should be used for trending. For example, you shouldn't automatically cut headcount if an area's expenses greatly exceed ABC costs for a given period. But, when you see it continually month after month, then you most likely have idle capacity and will need to manage this resource more closely. A partial list of other uses for ABM discussed in this book is shown below.

1. Cost Control/Expense Management

2. Capacity Management

3. Process Improvement

4. Staff Estimates

5. Activity Based Budgeting/Planning

Expenses versus Costs

The distinction between expenses and costs often gets blurred, but it is important to understand the difference. Expenses are what you find on the General Ledger. They are the physical bills paid by a corporation. For example, when a customer requests a service from a company certain activities will be performed to complete the request. These activities draw on the resources (equipment, personnel, office supplies, *etc.*) of a firm. Resources cost money and must be physically paid for (expenses). Payments for these expenses are recorded in the General Ledger.

Recording expenses is done using debits and credits on the General Ledger (GL). This is generally done on an organizational basis, at the departmental level. Expenses from the General Ledger are then used by accounting departments to prepare the financial statements given to shareholders. Expenses and their related General Ledger accounts are set up specifically to facilitate this. Therefore, "expenses" are meant for financial reporting, not for business and process improvement.

Most areas perform a variety of functions or services. Some services take more time and require more resources than others in the same area. This difference in usage means some functions cost more to perform than others. However, expenses are generally done at the department level in General Ledger, not at the functional level. Since only the net department amounts are recorded, this method of reporting makes it impossible to perform Product or customer profitability based on expenses. Therefore, expenses are not helpful in improving an organization and reporting detailed profitability. Expenses are valuable and necessary for financial reporting, but not for process improvement.

Costs are a translation of expenses into a format more reflective of the resources and efforts required by the different services. Unlike expenses, costs have no debit or credit components. Service costs are calculated based on the cost per resource and the amount of resources required. So, costs can be used for profitability reporting by Product, service, customer, or Business Unit. Costs also provide a meaningful view for process improvement and on-going management of resources.

Step One: Strategy and Goal Setting

The best way to strategize for ABM is to think big picture. Begin at the top by looking at the vision and goals of the company. *Yes, this sounds corny.* But, it is important to know in what direction the company is heading and in what area the company will be focusing its future growth on. This information will help your Activity Based Management Team focus your costing efforts on the right priorities. It will also help monitor the trends and design new processes to be efficient from the start. This will increase the profitability of the new service, decrease the amount of time it takes create the new process, and save a lot of rework. So, make sure you get in on the ground floor of any new projects or Products.

Some of your costing and improvement projects will be geared towards quality or regulatory requirements. However, most projects will be done to improve your company's metrics. So, the next step is to look at your company's metrics. Most business groups are given annual goals based on these metrics. Examples of metrics include ROA, ROE, Net Income, Sales per Employees, *etc*. Unfortunately, you can't manage a ratio. The calculation is what it is. But what you can do is manage and improve the numbers that make it up. So, the best approach is to reverse engineer the metric. This involves breaking a metric or ratio down into the components that make it up and looking for ways to positively affect those components.

For example, lets say a group at ABI is evaluated based on Return on Equity (ROE). Breaking the ratio down we see that it is Net Income (NI) divided by Common Stockholder Equity. Net Income is also a general term so we break it down more specifically as:

ROE = NI/Common Stockholder Equity, or

ROE = (Revenues - Expenses)/Common Stockholder Equity

Most people are narrowly focused on either revenue growth or expense reduction to improve their ROE. But, how about improving both. Or how about a stock repurchase? This would decrease Common Stockholder Equity, thereby improving the ratio. Or how about a combination of the three? So, just by looking at the components of the calculation you can brainstorm creative ways to improve the ROE.

Most process improvement projects focus on the expenses. On rare occasions, you may also be asked to tackle revenue growth as an Improvement project. However, you should probably avoid stock buy-backs projects (analyses). Stock repurchase can have both positive and negative impacts on many other ratios, taxes *etc*. So, that's a project best left for the financial professionals.

GOAL SETTING

Now lets look at a practical example of how to use reverse engineered metrics to set the goals for your Activity Based Management team. First, let's assume that Average Business Incorporated (ABI) has a goal of 18% ROE, and currently has revenues of $1,000,000, expenses of $900,000, and Common Equity of $1,000,000. These are some nice round numbers to illustrate this example.

Recall, ROE = (Revenues - Expenses)/Common Shareholder Equity. So, the current ROE is ($1,000,000 - $900,000)/$1,000,000 = 10%. The ABI Activity Based Management team wants to know how much they need to save through process improvements to help the corporation attain the target: 18%. So, they restate the calculation as:

Expenses = Revenues - (ROE * Common Shareholder Equity)

Or: Goal Expenses = Revenues - (Goal ROE * Common Shareholder Equity)

Assuming revenues and shareholder equity remain constant, you can fill in the data as follows:

Goal Expenses = $1,000,000 - (0.18 * $1,000,000) = $820,000

The team needs to make process improvements of $80,000 ($900,000 - $820,000) in order to increase the ROE from 10% to 18%. Taking this one step further they need to save over $6,666 per month through their improvement initiatives. Note: this is <u>actual</u> savings, not <u>identified</u> savings. Simply identifying improvements does not improve the financials or the ROE. The improvements must be implemented <u>and</u> the expenses reduced to recognize the $6,666 per month. As you'll learn later, reporting on and holding people accountable are two of biggest benefits of ABM.

Another way to look at improvements is by percentages. The team must reduce expenses by $80,000 or 8.9% ($80,000 divided by $900,000). So, each area of the bank must reduce their net expenses by at least 8.9%. Combining this with some revenue growth or a stock repurchase and ABI could easily exceed their ROE expectations.

Another example might involve Return on Assets (ROA). This ratio is calculated as (Revenues - Expenses)/Assets. Most people are narrowly focused on reducing their expenses to improve their ROA. Again, this works, but it is important to realize that both decreasing the assets and increasing the revenues will also improve the ratio. You need to consider this when performing any improvement project. Notice the following brainstorming illustration for Return on Assets (ROA):

Q: How do I decrease expenses?
A: Eliminate waste, increase productivity and decrease un-needed motions/transportation.

Q: How do I increase revenues?
A: Increase quality, decrease errors, decrease processing time, and keep Sales advised of: process improvements, increases in capacity, increases in quality, new services, *etc.* (basically anything Sales can use to differentiate your company from the competition).

Q: How can I decrease Assets?
A: Sell off un-needed equipment, decrease average inventory, reallocate fixed resources, *etc.*

The ROE and ROA analyses above are an example of reverse engineering. Taking the result and working backwards to find out how it works. Reverse engineering is an easy and important technique to learn since it can be used with any metric or measurement tool.

The ROE and ROA situations are excellent examples of how to use commonly available information to brainstorm ideas and set tangible targets for your Activity Based Management Team. You can find most of the targets above in the company's annual report, Stockholder Meeting minutes, interviews or articles with the CFO and CEO, the company newsletter and a variety of other sources.

The final thing you need to take into account when deciding where to focus you efforts is where management needs the help. Ask yourself: What Product lines are in trouble? Which areas cause the biggest headaches and waste the most amount of resources? Which items are an executive or manager's pet project (this may earn you a political ally later)? Not sure how to find the answers to these questions? Ask. There is plenty of organizational knowledge out there. All you have to do is ask. Now that you have a background of the environment *i.e.* where the company is going, how it is being measured and where management wants help, you are ready to start planning your project.

I can't emphasis enough, how important Strategy and Goal Setting are to having a successful Activity Based Management Team. ABM will tell you where you are, your goals tell you where you want to be and your process improvement projects are how you get there. Knowing your costs is not enough, the information must be actionable and action must be taken if you want to survive.

Step Two: Finding Resources

Most people want to use ABM on the entire corporation and affect change on a grand scale. That's natural. But, your available resources (namely: time, money, and manpower) will limit how much you can do. You will never have unlimited resources for Activity Based Management and there will always be constraints.

Some people would say: "you have to play with the hand you dealt". This phrase means you have to work within your constraints and with the resources you are given. But, that's not true. There are always options. Yes, you must start with the hand you are dealt (you have to start somewhere), but try thinking more strategically. It is crucial to think globally and work backwards. Think of what you'll need in the long run and begin setting this as an expectation. Think of it this way: "This is a good starting point, then as we move forward and build momentum over the next few years, we'll likely need to add resources." In other words, approach your resource challenges as you would a game of Poker or Black-jack 21. Focus on developing the hand you need rather than playing the hand you are dealt.

One way to estimate the resources you'll need is to use the one to one-fifty rule. For example, you usually need a ratio of 1:150 for staffing an Activity Based Management Team. This ratio means you need one Activity Based Management Tactician for every 150 employees. An Activity Based Management Tactician is responsible for several things:

1.   Calculating ABC costs

2.   Maintaining/updating ABC costs

3.   Analyzing processes

4.   Evaluating and recommending improvements for any given area

The ABM Tactician will also help the business area justify and submit capital expenditures for improvement projects and new processes. The 1:150 ratio will vary from company to company and even from area to area within the same company, but it's a good rule of thumb to start with.

Unfortunately, if your corporation has lots of employees (say 5,000), it will be difficult to justify the need to add 33 (5,000/150) new Activity Based Management Tacticians. You would also find it difficult to manage and coordinate 33 brand new employees at one time. So, your best bet is to start in one area of the firm with two or three outstanding Activity Based Management Tacticians. This approach will allow you to build some successes and get a better gauge on what the staffing ratio is like in your company.

A good gauge of success is whether you can save the company more than three times what your group earns every year. Great Activity Based Management Teams can often decrease expenses, increase revenues (or some combination of both) at rate of five times their salaries each year. Again, a goal to shoot for.

Start small, with just one area. Then as your team succeeds in that one, you can begin supporting a second area and so on. A string of successes will earn your group a shiny reputation. As this reputation grows, more areas will be asking for your help. The greater the demand for your services, the easier it will be to justify adding more Activity Based Management resources and human capital. See the Take Action section for more ideas on where to find help. Just remember: True success in ABM and process improvement is the accumulation of all the small successes.

Step Three: Define Products and Cost Drivers

Once you have the resources, you are ready to start working on your ABM system. The first step in any system design is to visualize the end-result. In our case the end result should be Activity Based Management. But, that's a broad target, so lets be more specific. How about: "A well-designed ABM system to track profitability, manage resources, and monitor on going expenses." Obviously we'd like to track this by Product or service, so the next step in designing an ABM system is to set up the list of Products and Cost Drivers you want to track.

PRODUCTS

Products are usually the easiest to define. Products are the core type of accounts or type of customers your corporation services. In banking and insurance it would be the type of account: Demand Deposit Account, Savings Account, Whole Life Insurance, Term Insurance, Trust, 401K, IRA, Certificate of Deposit, *etc*. Some of these can be broken down even further into Demand Deposit—Personal, Demand Deposit—Business, Personal Trust, Business Trust, *etc*. A consulting firm might consider the type of expertise provided: Technical Systems Consulting, Management Consulting, *etc*. Hospitals might consider Products to be the type of patient: Maternity, Emergency Room, Surgery, Out-patient Surgery, *etc*.

Most organizations already have a list of Products they use for profitability reporting. So, you may not need to create this from scratch. If your organization has one already, use that one as your starting point. It will be much easier to get buy-in that way.

COST DRIVERS

Cost Drivers are the means in which the Products are serviced. Cost Drivers are customer transactions or requests that cause (drive) activities to be performed in an Organization. Examples of Cost Drivers might be: Processing a Customer Order, Opening an Account, Originating a Loan, Processing a Deposit, Processing a Payment, *etc.* In a hospital, you might have: Complete an X-Ray, Triage Emergency Room Patient, Perform Routine Admittance, *etc.*

Cost Drivers are the cost points. Any type of service or transaction that you want to have a separate, unique cost should have a separate, unique Cost Driver. So, each of the drivers above would have a separate and unique cost. Each cost can be determined by looking at the components or chain of actions that are caused by the Cost Driver. For example, when a customer wants to open an account (Cost Driver) a whole sequence of activities will occur:

1. A sales associate helps the customer complete the application

2. The application is transported (sometimes electronically) to a processing area

3. The application is processed and approved

4. The customer is advised of approval

5. The account is set up on the computer system, *etc.*

Each of the actions above utilizes the company's resources thus costing the corporation time and money. The sum of all these actions is the cost of opening an account. Since the customer prompted all these actions by opening an account, "Open an Account" is the Cost Driver.

A sample Cost Driver table has been provided in Appendix A. The table shows the Cost Driver, unit of measure, definition, and data source. You should complete a table similar to this so you know exactly where the data comes from and what the results represent. Your actual table will vary, but this sample should give you a head start.

Cost Driver Rules of Thumb:

1. If it's a separate <u>sales channel</u> or customer <u>touch point</u>, then it should have its own Cost Driver. Notice in Appendix A there are separate Cost Drivers for many of the branch, ATM, and Internet transactions. This

allows you to compare costs across sales channels. You can then encourage/entice customers towards the least expensive channel for you to process.

2.   Do you want to be able to report on <u>unique</u> costs or to distinguish and report on certain types of a transaction (i.e. Initiate an Automated Payment versus Initiate a Payment Branch)? If so, then you will want to make separate Cost Drivers.

3.   <u>Keep it simple.</u> The more Cost Drivers you have the more you will have to maintain and update regularly. If the volume and total expense through the Cost Driver is negligible, then combine it into the "other" channel.

Tip:

If your Cost Drivers are sufficiently detailed, you may combine the Product and Cost Drivers. For example, you can create Cost Drivers such as Open a Home Equity Loan—Branch, Open a Home Equity Loan—Call Center, Open a Home Equity Loan—WEB, Open a Home Equity Loan—Other. In a sense, you are combining the Product list into an expanded Cost Driver list. The benefit is that you eliminate the need to maintain two separate lists (Products and Cost Drivers). The draw back is that you'll have many more Cost Drivers to look at.

SUB DRIVERS

Many ABM teams begin with a Cost Driver list like the sample provided. The Cost Drivers can also be broken into more detail by function. These are often referred to as Sub-Drivers. Sub-Drivers reflect the general processing steps that are required to complete the customer transaction (Cost Driver). Sub-Drivers are defined as you prepare for your time study. Similar to the Cost Drivers you will want to define what goes into the Sub-Drivers (the steps or activities). For example, if a customer wants to take out a loan, then "Originate a Loan" would be the Cost Driver. "Originate a Loan" would include the same basic steps as opening an account:

1.   A sales associate helps the customer complete the application

2. The application is transported (sometimes electronically) to a loan operations or processing department

3. The application is processed and approved

4. The customer is advised of approval

5. The account is set up on the computer systems, *etc.*

Each of these steps is a Sub-Driver for "Originate a Loan". The Sub-Drivers will likely occur across multiple departments and are the level at which the time study would be performed. On rare occasions, you may find it helpful to break down the Sub-Drivers into the individual activities that make it up. Hence, the term Activity Based Costing.

Tip:

Studying at a more detailed activity level is very time consuming and should be avoided when possible.

Using the costing techniques presented in this book, you will see how easy it is to conduct time studies and several alternative methods of measuring the ABC costs. After the cost study, you can then use your ABM system to roll up the costs to the higher-level Cost Drivers. Consider the example in Table 3.1 for Originating an Automobile Loan at Average Business Incorporated (ABI).

Table 3.1

Originate a Loan Process	Department	ABC Cost
Sub-Driver: Complete Application	Branch	$25.75
Sub-Driver: Mail to Loan Operations	Branch	$1.50
Sub-Driver: Process Application	Loan Ops	$2.25
Sub-Driver: Underwriter Approval	Underwriting	$6.75
Sub-Driver: Mail back to Branch	Underwriting	$1.50
Sub-Driver: Book Loan	Branch	$50.75
Sub-Driver: Mail to Loan Operations	Branch	$1.50
Cost Driver: Originate a Loan		$90.00

The sample ABC costs in Table 3.1 are based on time studies performed at a branch, loan operations, and underwriting at ABI. This simple report shows how much it costs to "Originate a Loan", what basic steps are included in the cost, and where the cost came from (department). It highlights that there is too much transportation to and from the retail branch. ABI would love to cut down on the cost by eliminating some of the transportation. Improving transportation might also improve turn-around times (possibly to same day) and decrease the risk of the application getting lost in the mail.

Obviously, they would only save $4.50 on transportation ($1.50 x 3) per loan originated. This amount doesn't sound like much, but the intangible benefits are far greater. An improvement such as this would make the company much more nimble. Without a lot of applications "in transit", ABI can adjust to market changes much more quickly. Faxing the application, using an on-line application submission/approval system, or giving ABI's sales folks approval power up to a pre-approved dollar level are several possible options to achieve this. These options are low hanging fruit—ripe and ready to pick (or fix).

Ideally, you should gather volume information on the Sub-Drivers on a regular basis. Unfortunately, it can be difficult, cumbersome or impractical to obtain automated data-sources for all the detailed Sub-Drivers. Sub-Driver volumes can also increase the amount of data to be stored up to ten fold. So, most teams use the Sub-Drivers for developing and analyzing ABC costs for process improvement, but not for reporting on-going profitability.

The next step is to look at the most expensive parts of the process (the big hitters). The ABM Team should seek-out a way to decrease these costs or simplify the processes. For Example ABI seeks a way to simplify the Application and Booking process. In this case, an on-line application process might save them some time and cost. So, on-line application submissions are a promising avenue to explore for capital investment.

At this point, it may sound like we're going off on a tangent. But, just in the last few minutes of reading, you can already see the power of ABM for profitability improvement. You can see what the costs are, what makes them up, and quickly brainstorm ways to improve the operation. With information like this, ABI might be able to change their name from the Average Business Incorporated to the Best of Breed Incorporated. But let's not get ahead of ourselves. They still need to find a way to put this together and make the information available to all employees. Now, that the group knows its goals, the corporation's strategy, and has defined the Products and Cost Drivers, they need to gather the volumes for the Cost Drivers and select a business area to focus their efforts on.

DATA SOURCES

One of the columns in the Cost Driver table is Data Source. Data Sources will vary from Product to Product and Cost Driver to Cost Driver. Some Cost Drivers may even have multiple data sources. For example opening an account might be done for a deposit account in the deposit account system, and in the lending system for a loan. This probably seems odd at first glance, but the Products are different (business checking versus business real estate loan). So different, that the systems used to manage them must be different.

Data Sources are where the transaction (Cost Driver) volumes are obtained on a recurring basis. Data Sources are often the core application and transaction systems where the transactions are processed and information is input or stored. ERP and management reporting systems are usually set up to automatically accumulate volumes and other statistics. These systems can make your life a lot easier. In fact, you will likely build your ABM system into them to leverage their power and end user penetration. A word of caution…when deciding where to get your data, remember GIGO (Garbage In = Garbage Out). Your goal is to be able to report profitability regularly or on a moment's notice. So, you want to be sure the Data Sources are reliable. If you allow your system to load in garbage data, then the output will also be garbage.

VOLUMES—WHAT ARE THEY AND WHERE TO FIND THEM?

Volumes represent the number of times a particular function or transaction is performed. Examples of this are Initiate a Payment, Initiate a Withdrawal, Initiate a Deposit, *etc.* These transactions draw on the firm's resources (labor, equipment, *etc.*). The consumption of resources based on transaction volumes forms the basis for transaction costs and profitability reporting. Therefore, volumes are an essential part of the costing and Activity Based Management.

Tip:

You will likely need volumes for every Cost Driver you have created and in some cases the Sub-Drivers. So the more Drivers you create, the more you have to find and maintain.

Volumes can be found in most information systems (Data Sources). For example, an Automated Teller System (for ATMs), records the number and type of each customer transaction. A Call Center system tracks the number of calls, type of inquiries, number of reservations, *etc.* Account Management systems count the number of accounts in force, number of transactions, account types, *etc.* Customer Relationship Information systems track customer statistics such as customer name, related accounts, sales executive name, customer address, credit rating, *etc.* The list goes on and on. You can draw on any or all of these systems depending on what you are looking for. See Appendix A for sample Data Sources by Cost Driver.

How it Works

Automated application systems usually assign codes to each customer transaction based on the type of activity. For example, in ABI's ATM system you might see transaction codes such as 101, 102, and 103. Pulling (extracting) the data from the system you would see something like Table 3.2.

Table 3.2

Account Number	Transaction Code	Transaction Amount
1234	101	$20.00
1234	102	$0.00
1234	103	$50.00

The transaction codes in the extract file (Table 3.2) are meaningless to the layperson. Therefore, each Data Source's transaction codes must be mapped to Cost Drivers as shown in Table 3.3.

Table 3.3

Transaction Code	Cost Driver
101	Initiate an ATM Withdrawal
102	Initiate an ATM Inquiry
103	Initiate an ATM Deposit

This mapping process is often referred to as the data mapping and can be recorded in a data dictionary. You may find that several transaction codes should be included in one Cost Driver. This is usually true if the ABC costs are the same for several transactions or the volume of a few of the transactions is very small. Then, through your Activity Based Management System you can summarize the customer transactions as shown in Table 3.4.

Table 3.4

Account Number	Cost Driver	Volume	Amount
1234	Initiate an ATM Withdrawal	1	$20.00
1234	Initiate an ATM Inquiry	1	$0.00
1234	Initiate an ATM Deposit	1	$50.00

Many automated systems may already be linked to your management reporting system. In fact, many of the transaction volumes you want may already be there. So collecting this data may not be as daunting a task as it appears. If a function or transaction is recorded in or performed by a computer, there is a good chance you can get the volume. You just have to ask the right questions to the right people. Since you already know what you are looking for (Cost Driver list), finding volumes will be much easier. 90% of business today is information based. The information is out there. In fact, you'll usually find you have more data than you know what to do with. It is just a matter of how to narrow it down to the most useful items.

OTHER STATISTICS

You can also get statistics on a number of other useful items. These may include: the number of applications, ratio of applications taken to loans booked, ratio of reservation inquiries to actual reservations booked, amount of system resources utilized for different computer processes, *etc.* In short, you can get almost any metric the company measures.

Gathering other statistics or metrics will also make your Activity Based Management system much more robust and valued. "Dollarizing" the ratios and statistics as part of your costing analysis is also beneficial. For example, what is the cost of processing applications for loans that are never booked? How can you minimize that cost? What is the cost of processing, then rejecting an application for a loan and how can you minimize that cost? What is the cost of rework on applications and how can you decrease that? What is the cost of answering an inquiry for a property, but not making a sale and how do you improve those marks?

Tip:

If you are not sure where or whom to ask to get the volume, start with the people who are actually performing the transaction. Often they know whom to call if the system is down. That's usually the help desk. The help desk will know where and from whom you can get the volume.

Tip:

Not sure what volumes and statistics to gather? Ask the department managers how they track Productivity and what they are measured on. Then ask where those measurements come from, who generates them and how you can get an automatic feed.

Tip:

When the metrics are manually calculated, see if you can develop a report to calculate this automatically. Manual reports are a pain. Automated reports eliminate the headaches, increase data consistency, and save people time.

Tip:

Once you find a good source for the volume and have validated it against actual transactions, you should automate the process of volume collection. You may be gathering these statistics from many sources simultaneously, so automation will save you a lot of time and maintenance. You are in the business of process improvement not volume generation. Let the computer do the grunt work.

Step Four: Select an Area to Study

It is often better to try to improve a process than an organization. Improving an organization can be taken personally. People get defensive about their "fiefdoms". They feel like someone is looking over their shoulders and they don't like prying eyes and un-solicited criticism. Approaching it as a "process" improvement is a more readily accepted approach. Let managers know that this is one of many areas in the study. Emphasize that you are there to help them identify and <u>implement</u> improvements in the process. It is a collaborative approach to problem solving, not an audit. This approach is often more positively received and <u>constructive</u> help (unlike criticism) is always welcome.

A good place to start is in the processing areas. Processing areas typically perform the same repetitive activities or steps. Try starting with an area that has only one or two main services. This type of department is easily recognized by mapping out the activities it performs. For example, lets say the Activity Based Management Team at ABI is asked to look at the Auto Loan. Their first step would be to start with an overall Life Cycle flow chart (yes, this is where it comes in handy).

MAPPING THE PROCESS

It is best to begin mapping (LCC flow) at a high level, then work downwards to develop the details. Someone familiar with the overall process, such as the Product Manager, can help you with the initial process steps. For example, an account is opened, it is supported, and it is closed as shown in the Figure 4.1.

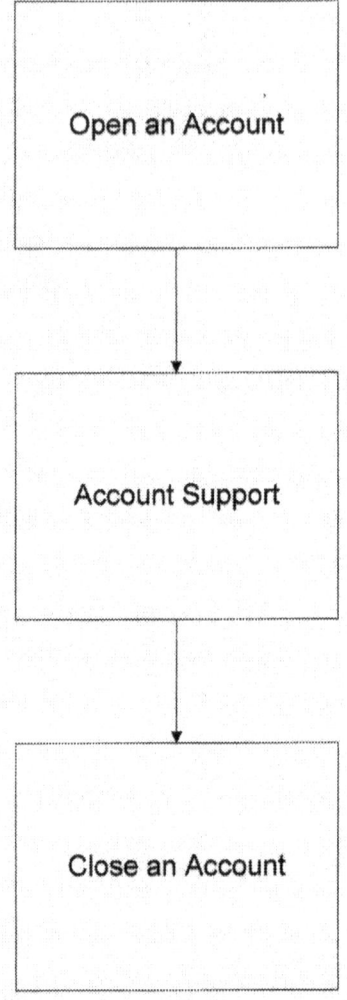

Figure 4.1

Opening and Closing Accounts are more of a sales based analysis, which we'll discuss later. Right now, we are focused on operational improvements so we'll zero in on Account Support. Account Support involves updating customer information, processing payments, processing late payment fees, and processing statements. So, we break it down into its component parts as shown in Figure 4.2.

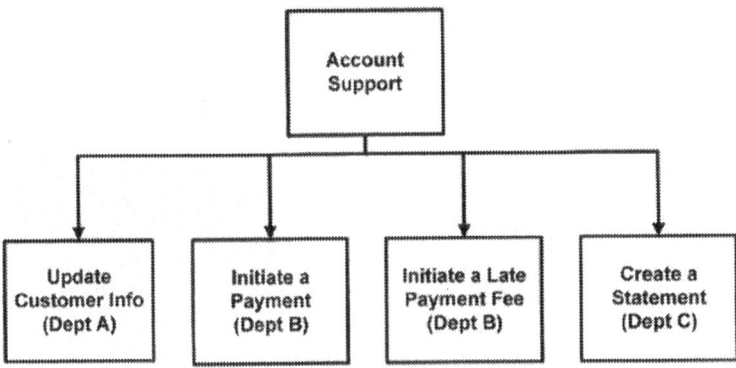

Figure 4.2

Notice in Figure 4.2 that we have also incorporated the departments into the chart, so we know where the cost of each function is derived. The department information is readily found by asking the Product Manager or anyone else familiar with the Product and the processes that support it. It is usually not possible to list departments at the higher level (Account Support) because the term is so broad. The support actions required on a regular basis are done through a variety of departments. The component parts in Figure 4.2 are the Cost Drivers. Incorporating the detail into the original chart (Figure 4.1), you have more detailed view of the Product's Life Cycle.

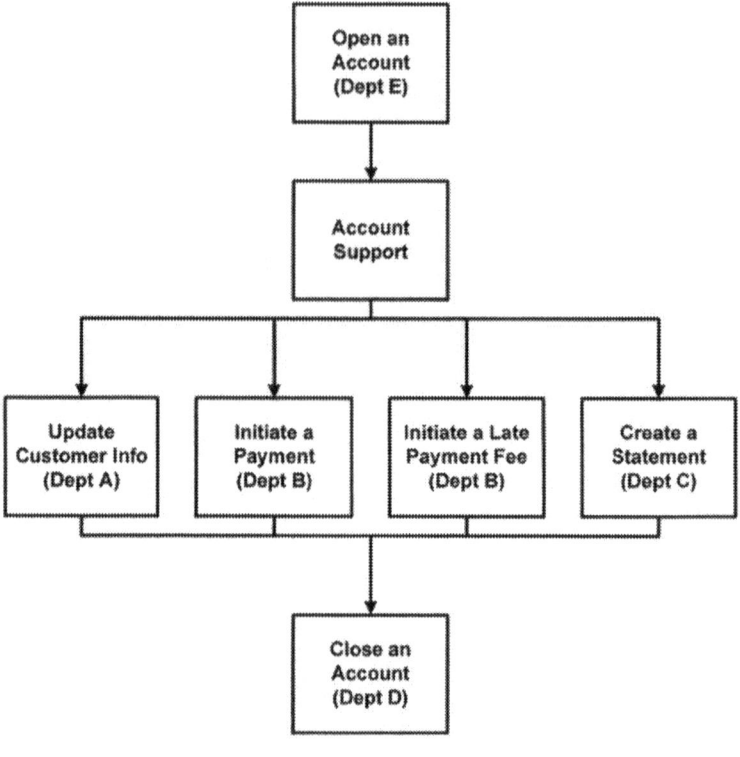

Figure 4.3

Some transactions involve multiple departments. For example, Initiate a Payment may go through multiple departments (B, H and I). In that case, you can break it down even further into the Sub-Driver to define how each department contributes to successful completion of the process. This is shown below.

1. Accept payment and payment coupon—Department H (Branch)

2. Forward payment and coupon to Back Office Operations—Department H (Branch)

3. Payment processed and customer account adjusted—Department B (Back Office Operations)

4. Loan application system updated to reflect new balance—Department I (Information Systems)

After breaking Account Support down into its component parts and assigning responsibility departments, you are now ready to plan your ABC study. You do this by selecting which departments to study first and in what order.

SELECTING A STUDY AREA

One way to select a study area is to look at the dollar impact. First review the Lifecycle—charts developed above with Product Management or someone familiar with the Product. You want to make sure you've interpreted the process correctly and you are not chasing phantom costs (costs that are perceived to exist, but do not). Then, with a little research, you can find the total expenses for each of the departments.

Table 4.1

Responsibility Area	Monthly Expense
Department A	$55,000
Department B	$150,000
Department C	$96,000
Department D	$50,000
Department E	$73,000
Total	**$424,000**

Some people like to annotate the expenses directly on the Life Cycle Chart. This annotation is misleading, since each of these areas may support multiple Products and services, not just the one on your Life Cycle Chart. For example, Department B at ABI supports Payments and Late Processing Fees for many Products not just Auto Loans. If you truly want to place it in the chart, put it as a footnote in the bottom right hand corner.

Armed with the expenses and flow chart, the Activity Based Management Team is now ready to prioritize where they will begin their ABC studies. The Product Manager and Business Unit (BU) Executive are most concerned about departments B and C. They feel there is a lot of opportunity for savings in those departments and they should be the easiest place to standardize the processes. The Activity Based Management Team agrees. They realize that improving departments B and C will give the information an immediate audience within management and account for the two largest expense departments (over 58% of the total).

Selecting where to begin can be critical to the success of your overall project. The first couple of departments may be a little challenging. So, you want to use them as an opportunity to learn. You want to learn and refine your ABM skills early on. Then leverage the best techniques to use on future studies.

Tip:

It is crucial to sit down as a team after each new study or major project and conduct an After Project Review (APR) session. APRs are used to brainstorm what went well and what did not. You can document these items and use them to help the team learn from its mistakes and brainstorm ways to improve in the future. Essentially, you are looking for ways to improve your processes. APRs make future projects faster, cleaner and more professional. They help you avoid making the same mistakes twice and provide a training source for new employees to prevent them from making the same mistakes as their predecessors.

You also want to get a string of successful improvements. A string of successes will help build your team's confidence (Success Breeds Success). Success in the first few areas will give you the confidence and clout to carry this process on to other areas. So, pick your target carefully. Don't begin your first study in the most difficult area or with the most complex Products, that would spell certain disaster.

Tip:

Use this book as guide. So first, think about your vision of the future. Decide where you want to go, what you want the result to look like, and how the results will be used. Next, make a project plan, and implement it on an easy area. This approach will allow you to fine-tune the plan (using APRs as mentioned above) before you tackle bigger and more complex areas.

Other factors to consider when prioritizing departments are:

- Headcount
- Volume
- Areas with decreasing Productivity or increasing expenses

- Areas with highest number of complaints

- Areas that cause the highest amount of aggravation, problems, *etc.*

Examining the list above, the Activity Based Management Team also asks for input about what sort of challenges are being faced by the organization. They are looking for other ways to add value with study. If all the team does is calculate costs, then no immediate value is provided to the department. In fact, a separate study would need to be done later for process improvement. It is more efficient and less intruding to provide a one-stop service rather than interrupt the employee's work process two or more times. So, the ABM Team wants to work with management to develop costs, solve existing problems, <u>and</u> improve processes to meet long-term strategy of the corporation.

Step Five: Calculate Activity Times

The basic calculation for ABC and ABM is: Volume * ABC cost. Both items (ABC cost and volume) must be gathered and calculated by Cost Driver to populate the ABC data and feed the Activity Based Management system. We have already discussed the volumes and where to find them. The ABC costs are based on the activity times so we will discuss how to get the activity time first.

TRADITIONAL TIME-STUDY TECHNIQUE

Activity times are developed using time studies. Traditionally this involves defining the Sub-Drivers (tasks) performed for the Cost Driver in a given department, then timing each of these activities and rolling them up to the Cost Driver level for that department. The sum of the Cost Driver times across all the departments is the Cost Driver's total activity time. The activity time, and the detail that makes it up, is important because it can be used as a benchmark for process improvement. So keep good notes on what the time is and what actions/steps are included in it.

As part of a process improvement project, the analysis can be broken into activity level detail. The activity level can be rather detailed and cumbersome. For example, breaking the "Initiate a Payment" function at the activity level would resemble Table 5.1.

Table 5.1

Department B	Activity Time	Position Title
Open Mail and forward to Processors	35 sec	Mail Clerk
Review coupon and check	12 sec	Processor
Process Payment	25 sec	Processor

Table 5.1 (Continued)

Department B	Activity Time	Position Title
Initiate a Payment Subtotal	1 min 12 sec (0.0200 hrs/item) (50 items/hour)	

This type of analysis can be done at the either the activity level or the Sub-Driver level. Remember, the more detailed your breakouts in the system, the more functions you'll need to time and maintain. Don't get too detailed. Notice in Table 5.1 that the position title of the person responsible for the activity is also recorded. Recording the position helps to look for time wasted in queues and hand-offs. Hand-offs create opportunities for documents to be missed, over-looked or lost. Hand-offs can also cause information to be miss-communicated or forgotten.

In this example, the mail function can be used for multiple Cost Drivers. Thus, it makes sense that one person takes care of the mail function and forwards material on to the appropriate or next available processor. The position title, activity, and department can be utilized for other process improvement techniques such as swim lanes. Lastly, it is important to state the time in both minutes/seconds and in decimal hours. The minutes and seconds are more readable to the end user when looking at the activity time. Decimal hours come in handy for follow-on analysis and calculations such as headcount estimating, unused capacity, *etc.* which are all done in [decimal] hours.

The activity times shown in Table 5.1 are generally developed through time studies using a stopwatch. This entails observing the employee perform the activity, then timing the employee for a number of repetitions. Timing a larger number of repetitions is generally preferred in order to get a statistically valid sample.

How many repetitions should be timed?

Don't go overboard. There are many books and web sites on the Internet that can help you determine the required number of repetitions. You can also calculate the number of observations required using some basic statistics. In essence, it all boils down to the variance of your sample, the level of confidence desired, and your acceptable error margin. The more consistent the activity times and the larger your acceptable range of error, the less trials you'll need to get a sample that is representative of the overall population. However, this is not a statistics book so we'll leave it at that.

There will be fluctuations in the activity times from transaction to transaction in any time study. But when looking at the samples as a whole the manager usually has a good feel for how long it normally takes. Often the ABM Team will time the activities for a given day, and then review the results with the manager. Validation with the manager ensures that the times are reasonable and representative. The times developed here will be used to benchmark process improvement. They will also be used for evaluating the performance of the group and for ABC costing. So obtaining buy-in from the manager is crucial.

Tip:

Set up the activities and do some initial observations on a slow day. This allows the Activity Based Management Tactician plenty of time to interact with the employees and refine the tasks. Then perform the actual timing on one or more busy days. Timing on a busy day will give you a truer picture of what the employees are capable of and can repeat over long periods (i.e. allowing for personal fatigue and downtime).

What activities should be timed?

As you observe the area and talk with the employees, you'll find that a sub-set of the activities accounts for 80–85% of their time. Those activities should be timed. The remainder should be defined for later use in process improvement, but can be listed as other for the purposes of the activity times.

The traditional (easiest) method to get the activity times is using a stopwatch. You simply define the activities/steps and time them using a standard stopwatch. As you record each trial, you get a good sense as to what a reasonable time would be. Once you've completed timing the trials you can then run it by the manager and agree on a reasonable time for the activity.

Tip:

Timing for longer periods and for a larger number of repetitions on a busy day will generally yield better results.

This is a very simple, traditional time-study technique that most people are familiar with. However, several other techniques that have recently become popular. These techniques include MTM, Bar Coding, Tick Sheets, Surveys, *etc.* These methods can be significant time savers, so each is mentioned briefly below.

NON-TRADITIONAL TIME-STUDY TECHNIQUES

MTM—Methods Time Measurement

MTM is very reliable and has been around for quite a while. It is based on countless time motion studies done over the past 50 years. The premise of this method is that every motion (reach, grab, stand, sit, walk, *etc.*) takes a set amount of time. Combine this with the distance traveled, weight carried, resistance applied etc., and you have a reliable estimate of the time for each movement. The sum total of these motion times is the total time it would take a normal person to perform a task for an extended period.

The reason MTM is still valid and in use today is that the human body hasn't evolved much over the last 50 years. We haven't grown new appendages; we still have two eyes, two hands, and walk upright. Thus, our basic range of motions hasn't changed. In fact, being tried and tested for over 50 years has allowed industry to improve and fine-tune the technique for use in other endeavors including workspace design and ergonomics. Thus, MTM has become a very scientific and statistically valid approach.

You develop an MTM activity time by observing and documenting the motions of a particular task. Then you can look up the activity time for each of these motions on an MTM chart and come up with a standard time. The nice part about this technique is that you can look for wasted motions and help employees become more efficient in their work tasks. MTM also lends itself well to ergonomic improvements and analyzing ergonomic risk factors.

Many people like this method because you can use the list of motions to estimate the activity time of a new or proposed process. This step can save you a lot of time and money. You can also copy the motions from one task to another. There are many computer programs that can help you develop MTM and there are several large and loyal user groups. So, assistance and advice is plentiful.

The drawbacks of this method are buy-in and attention to detail. MTM is very detailed and many people are initially skeptical about using it. The level of detail involved in this method requires you to be very meticulous about writing down the motions you observe. It takes some practice to become proficient at breaking down the motions and identifying the core movements, but it is not rocket science.

Tip:

The easiest way to get buy-in on this method is with a practical example. Do a few trials for a given task, both with a stopwatch and using MTM. Then compare the times. If done correctly, the results will be nearly the identical.

Bar Coding

Bar Coding allows one Activity Based Management Tactician to time multiple employees at the same time. You simply provide each employee with a barcode scanner and barcodes for each of the activities the employee performs. The employee then scans the appropriate bar code each time he performs a task. The barcode reader stores the information for later analysis. Alternatively, some scanners communicate wirelessly with a base station for "real-time" results. Over the course of several days, you can get a very good statistical sampling using this method.

The drawback of bar coding is that it is a little time consuming to define the tasks, set up the bar codes, and conduct the time study. The employees may also require a little time to get used to the new technology and scanning the bar codes. Finally, we're all human. Mistakes will be made. Consequently, you'll need some way to edit the data or over-ride what was recorded when mistakes are found.

Some groups have installed the bar codes as part of their regular work processes. This allows them to monitor the work on an on-going basis, evaluate real-time Productivity, and constantly monitor the validity of the activity times. It also allows you to compare times across employees and teams for Productivity, downtime, *etc.*

Another variation is bar-coding the work itself as it enters the area. Each employee scans the item as it enters their workstation and scans it again as it is completed or leaves the area. This information can be used for tracking productivity and wait (queue) times. It can also provide real-time tracking for customer applications, requests, payments, *etc.* See Automated Systems Section to see how to use this kind of data for activity times.

Tick Sheets

Tick Sheets can be used when an employee performs the same function through-out the day or for an extended time-period. Tick Sheets are sheets of paper on which employees record the number of times a transaction occurs. Employees do this by placing tick marks on the sheet each time the activity is performed. Then, at the end of the time-period you divide the hours worked by the number ticks on the sheet. The result is the average activity time. This is similar to what is called Average Costing since it's a simple division of total hours divided by the volume. Tick Sheets are manual, so they require a level of responsibility and integrity on the employee's part.

Using Tick Sheets also reinforces the need to do this on a busy day. A popular theory that holds true in many situations is Parkinson's Law. Simply stated, the amount of time it takes to perform a task will increase to fill the time available for it. So if a person has the capability of completing 500 payments per eight-hour day, but only receives 400 payments a day. In the long run, the amount of time it takes to initiate a payment will increase until the 400 payments consume his full eight-hour day.

Tip:

Often Tick Sheet counts can be found on system generated reports. This would eliminate the need for the employee to record the number of occurrences. Sample reports include: Daily Error Reports, Daily Transaction Reports, Data Entry Reports, Reconcilement Reports, Daily Adjustment Reports, *etc.*

Surveys

Surveys are another easy way to get a rough idea of the time spent on different tasks. Surveys are exactly like they sound and are often used by consultants. You survey the employees to find out what activities they perform and how much of their time (either in hours or as a percentage of total time) is spent on those tasks. Then you divide the time by the task volume to get an average activity time per task. The activity time can also be converted to an ABC cost to gauge the dollar impact of the tasks performed.

Surveys are similar to Tick Sheets because it establishes an average Cost (total hours/task volume). Surveys are also simple to design and complete. Some organizations design the survey and print it out for employees to complete. Others do it through e-mail or over the company's Intranet (or internet). The advantage of doing it electronically is that the results are near real time. Reports can also be designed to assist supervisors in seeing who has completed the survey and who hasn't. This eliminates one of the common aggravations for the Activity Based Management Team of reporting on and tracking down individuals that haven't completed the survey. Another advantage is that you can summarize the information from the electronic survey and export it to a spreadsheet or another program for more customized reports. In comparison, surveys done on paper must be collected and the data entered manually before any results can be analyzed.

Drawbacks of Surveys and Tick Sheets

Most people, consultants included, like surveys because they are quick and easy. They help you identify where the time is spent and opportunities for improvement. However, surveys and Tick Sheets are generally not used for on-going costing. The reason is that surveys assume 100% of the time is occupied or consumed. You are assuming that there is no idle capacity. This assumption is contradictory to Activity Based Costing and causes several serious side effects. For example, consider survey results for an average employee at ABI shown in Table 5.2.

Table 5.2

Activity	% of Time Spent	Total Hours	Volume	Activity Time (Hours)	Activity Time (HH:MM:SS)
Transaction Processing	50%	1,040.0	100	10.4000	10:24:00
Update Customer Account	35%	728.0	1,500	0.4853	0:29:07
Close Account	15%	312.0	500	0.6240	0:37:26
Total	**100%**	**2,080.0**			

Table 5.2 highlights the fact that departmental employees spend a lot of time updating customer accounts. In essence, the employee spends an average of 728 hours per year performing updates. The department manager is not surprised by the survey results. But he is concerned that his area spends so much time updating accounts. He knows that some paper work and account updates are required.

However, he'd like to have his department spend more time processing transactions.

So, he asks the Activity Based Management Team to undertake a project to decrease the Update Customer Account time. Through process improvements, the team was able to decrease the average activity time from 29 minutes per account to 12 minutes. The improvement was accomplished through employee training, system automation, and a few information system enhancements. Everyone is pleased and the department now focuses the extra time on transaction processing.

A few months later the department manager wants to see how things are progressing, so he asks for another survey. The department manager knows that the transaction volume has increased due to increased emphasis on processing work and wants to see the resulting activity times. The results of the updated survey are shown in Table 5.3.

Table 5.3

Activity	% of Time Spent	Total Hours	Volume	Activity Time (Hours)	Activity Time (HH:MM:SS)
Transaction Processing	70%	1,456.0	130	11.2000	11:12:00
Update Customer Account	15%	312.0	1,500	0.2080	0:12:28
Close Account	15%	312.0	500	0.6240	0:37:26
Total	100%	2,080.0			

The department manager was shocked. The volumes increased as expected and the activity time for Update Customer Account decreased. However, the activity times for Transaction Processing increased and the resulting ABC cost increased. How could this be?

The results of the second survey highlight one of the flaws with the surveys and tick sheets. Tick sheets and surveys assume that 100% of the time is fully utilized. Thus, by decreasing the time spent in one area, you will increase the time spent on others. Also, recall that the activity time is simply the total hours divided by the total volume. So, to compensate for the increase in total processing hours, the volume must increase at an equal or greater rate. If it doesn't, an increased average activity time will result. In this case, the volume must increase to 140 for

Transaction Processing just to breakeven! The breakeven calculations are shown below.

Table 5.4

Task	New Hours	/	Old Activity Time	=	Break-Even Volume
Transaction Processing	1,456.0	/	10.4000	=	140

This simple calculation shows that, given the process improvements, the volume of transactions will need to increase by 40% (from 100 to 140 transactions processed). Notice how this coincides with an increase in the amount of time spent on each of those activities. So, if you plan to increase the percentage of time spent on processing by 40% (from 50% to 70%), then the volume must increase by the same rate (40%) in order to breakeven on the activity times and ABC costs.

The second problem with using surveys and tick sheets for on going costing is that they are volume sensitive. Transaction volumes fluctuate over time, which will cause the activity times to fluctuate. Consider the survey below, which was performed one year after the original survey.

Table 5.5

Activity	% of Time Spent	Total Hours	Volume	Activity Time (Hours)	Activity Time (HH:MM:SS)
Transaction Processing	50%	1,040.0	70	14.8571	14:51:25
Update Customer Account	35%	728.0	3,000	0.2427	0:14:33
Close Account	15%	312.0	1500	0.2080	0:12:28
Total	100%	2,080.0			

The percentage of time spent by the employee, as shown in Table 5.5, is the same. However, comparing the activity times to the original survey you find that as the volume increases the activity time decreases. Likewise, as the volume decreases, the activity time increases. Clearly, surveys are volume sensitive. This volume-based change makes the department appear more or less efficient, when in fact no change in the process has occurred. The same tasks are performed to update an account this year as the last. Yet, the tasks appear to take more or less time than before. A comparison of two surveys is shown in Table 5.6.

Table 5.6

Activity	Original Volume	New Volume	Original Activity Time (HH:MM:SS)	New Activity Time (HH:MM:SS)	% Change in Activity Time
Transaction Processing	100	70	10:24:00	14:51:25	43%
Update Customer Account	1,500	3,000	0:29:07	0:14:33	-50%
Close Account	500	1,500	0:37:26	0:12:28	-67%

Conducting surveys and using tick sheets during periods of low volumes can also pose hazards to your costing. Lower than normal volumes result in the same hours being divided by a smaller volume. This condition causes the activity times to increase, the ABC costs to be inflated, and the price charged to the customer to increase.

The last problem with using surveys for on going costing is in reporting. Surveys assume 100% of the time is allocated. You are assuming there is no unused or idle capacity. This assumption is incorrect. Unfortunately, surveys do not show idle capacity. They don't show how much additional volume or how many more customers can be serviced given the current amount of resources. You could try to add a factor into surveys for idle capacity, say 15%. But this is difficult to do because idle capacity fluctuates over time. Additionally, one of the major reasons for doing ABM is to monitor and minimize idle capacity, not to assume one.

In short, the examples above show how activity times derived from Surveys are inappropriate for costing. This is not to say that Surveys are not useful for process improvement. They are. Surveys are an excellent way to quickly summarize the work performed in a department and highlight opportunities to improvement. Surveys can also be a quick method for populating initial (benchmark) ABC costs. However, they should not be used for on-going costing and Activity Based Management.

Other Portable Devices (PDAs, Mobile Computers etc.)

Today there are many popular portable devices on the market (i.e. Palm Pilots, Pocket PCs, Lap Top Computers and Tablet PCs). These devices can be huge time savers for Activity Based Management Teams. Best of all they are small and portable. You can take them anywhere for data collection and real time analysis.

Portable devices are an easy way to track activity times. You can do this by purchasing software or by building your own custom forms and macros. The data can even be exported into a database for storage and reporting in the ABM system. Best of all, the data is collected real time. So, it is a convenient tool to spot check times for reasonableness with the employee or supervisor. This is a very simple concept, but you can easily build in more features for Six Sigma, TQM, ergonomics *etc.* The best thing is that you don't have to go back to your office to type in all the data, summarize, and create the statistics. You've got it real-time and the software only takes a few hours to develop.

Another neat trick is to populate a small database with MTM baseline data. You can develop a program where the ABM Tactician can click on each MTM motion as it occurs. Then the program rolls up the data and exports it to a spreadsheet for analysis and reporting.

Videotaping

There are many options for gathering and visually recording study information. PDAs, Pocket PCs, palm sized cameras, digital recorders, and traditional video cameras to name a few. There are several benefits with visual recording devices. First, you have a visual record of the activities that were studied. A visual record that allows you replay and review the activities to ensure you've documented and timed them correctly. Many devices even allow you to display the time on the screen and hit pause when necessary to examine the situations in more detail.

Videotaping is also well suited for MTM. Organizations that are new to MTM can pause, replay and review the video as often as necessary. This feature ensures each motion is noted and recorded in the study data. The visual record can then be stored on tapes, CDs, DVDs or even placed on a centralized server and attached to the study data file for easy reference.

The second benefit of videotaping is that it minimizes the Hawthorne affect. Simply stated, when people know they are being watched they tend to work harder or better. This change in worker habits skews traditional time study results. However, in the long run people tend to fall back to their usual habits. Thus, videotaping can be done over the course of several shifts or several days to negate the Hawthorne Effect. This expanded time can give you a truer picture of what employees are capable of over the long run.

The third benefit of videotaping is process improvement. Work teams can review the videos and look for ways to become more efficient. You can also use it to benchmark those employees or processes that consistently achieve the highest results. Video-taping allows teams to review the process step by step, pausing to discuss what went well, and what can be improved within the process.

Finally, videotaping allows an ABM Practitioner to time and observe several people, functions or activities in a one area at the same time. Then the ABM Team can review the video afterwards and time each of the activities shown on the video. You can also record video in one area while simultaneously doing a traditional time study in another. Obviously, this can be a real lifesaver when you are trying to capture activities that seldom occur.

Automated Systems

Automated systems provide an unprecedented wealth of activity time and Activity Based Management Information. These systems track how long transactions take, errors generated, amount of system resources utilized, *etc*. Such systems might include communication network systems, order entry systems, call center systems, internet reservation systems, *etc*. Table 5.7 shows an example of a transaction log from an automated system.

Table 5.7

	Start Time
Employee login	7:00:01 AM
Transaction A	7:00:15 AM
Transaction B	7:01:24 AM
Transaction A	7:01:50 AM
Transaction A	7:02:45 AM
Transaction C	7:03:52 AM
Transaction B	7:04:45 AM
Transaction C	7:05:12 AM

Table 5.7 (Continued)

	Start Time
Transaction A	7:06:13 AM
Transaction A	7:09:42 AM
Transaction B	7:10:46 AM
Transaction C	7:11:10 AM

From this Automated Source you can quickly calculate the sample times as shown in Table 5.8.

Table 5.8

	Start Time	Duration (Sample Activity Time)
Employee login	7:00:01 AM	0:00:14
Transaction A	7:00:15 AM	0:01:09
Transaction B	7:01:24 AM	0:00:26
Transaction A	7:01:50 AM	0:00:55
Transaction A	7:02:45 AM	0:01:07
Transaction C	7:03:52 AM	0:00:53
Transaction B	7:04:45 AM	0:00:27
Transaction C	7:05:12 AM	0:01:01
Transaction A	7:06:13 AM	0:03:29
Transaction A	7:09:42 AM	0:01:04
Transaction B	7:10:46 AM	0:00:24
Transaction C	7:11:10 AM	0:00:51

Then sort by Transaction and Duration to get a rough idea of how much time each transaction takes.

Table 5.9

	Time	Duration (Sample Activity Time)
Transaction A	7:01:50 AM	0:00:55
Transaction A	7:09:42 AM	0:01:04
Transaction A	7:02:45 AM	0:01:07
Transaction A	7:00:15 AM	0:01:09
Transaction A	7:06:13 AM	0:03:29
Transaction B	7:10:46 AM	0:00:24
Transaction B	7:01:24 AM	0:00:26
Transaction B	7:04:45 AM	0:00:27
Transaction C	7:11:10 AM	0:00:51
Transaction C	7:03:52 AM	0:00:53
Transaction C	7:05:12 AM	0:01:01

At a glance, Transaction A takes roughly 1 minute 7 seconds; Transaction B takes 26 seconds and Transaction C 53 seconds. These are the activity times the Activity Based Management Team will select. You can calculate an average activity time for each transaction. However, average times would have the same problems inherent in surveys (i.e. total time divided by the volume). So, ABM Teams and department managers normally select a representative time as shown above.

Notice also that the last sample of Transaction A took over 3 minutes. Looking back at Table 5.8 this is either an abnormally long transaction or it includes wait time in between transactions. Since the rest of the times are consistent for Transaction A, it safe to assume that this is an abnormality and can be ignored. If there were a lot of abnormalities in the activity times, then more research would need to be done.

Tables 5.7 through 5.9 reflect a small sampling (11 minutes) out of one employee's day. Imagine combining the results of all the employees, for the entire day. That would create an amazing sample. The main benefit is that you don't have to distract employees from servicing their customers. It is all done behind the scenes. Just run the numbers and review the results with the manager for buy-in. Similar to bar coding, this method can be done continuously or spot-checked over time. Continuous monitoring provides real-time data on productivity and allows you to benchmark the top performing teams.

Step Six: Calculate ABC Costs

Once your activity times are calculated (using one of the methods above), you are ready to convert the activity times (in decimal hours) to an ABC cost. The two basic methods for accomplishing this are the Hourly Rate Method and the Resource Costing Method. First, it is prudent to review the concept of fixed and variable costs since they play an integral part in the ABC cost calculations and the usage of this information.

FIXED COSTS

All costs can be divided into two categories fixed or variable. Fixed costs are those that do not vary over time or do not vary within a certain range of volumes. Such costs might include: exempt labor, machine depreciation and occupancy. For example if you have a manager for given department, the manager is paid the same amount each time period regardless of the volume and demand for services from that department. Likewise for machine depreciation and occupancy. The costs will be the same amount each period, regardless of the fluctuations in the number of transactions.

Fixed costs generally do not change unless there is a significant change in demand. For example, if the volume increases by a large amount, more equipment capacity may need to be added. Adding new equipment will obviously increase the depreciation cost by the number of machines added. Therefore, the fixed costs move in a step pattern following the equipment capacity as shown in Figure 6.1 below.

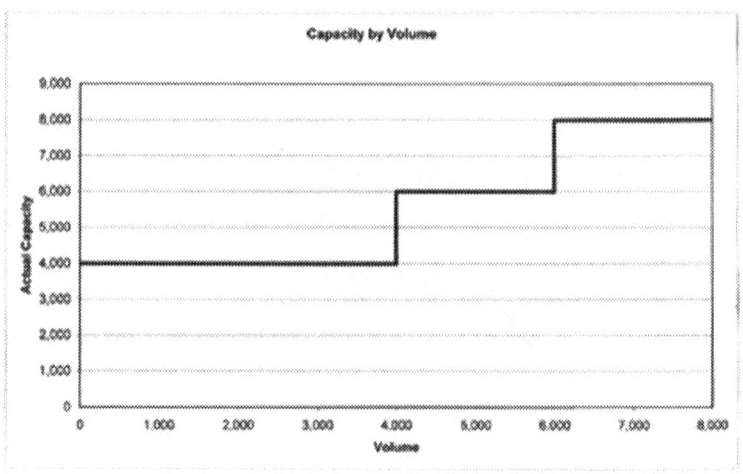

Figure 6.1

This graph shows the department originally has 2 machines capable of handling 2,000 transactions each (4,000 transactions total). As the demand for services (volume) increases from 3,000 to 4,000, the department's machines will become fully loaded and leave no extra time for repairs or maintenance. Then the department must add a third machine. In this case adding a third machine would increase the total capacity to 6,000 transactions (3 machines x 2,000 transactions per machine). Buying a third machine will obviously increase in the depreciation costs as well.

One of the main benefits of Activity Based Management is knowing how much idle capacity your company has. Idle capacity can be used to calculate potential room for business expansion, the reallocation of under-utilized resources to areas that are over capacity, and improving operational costs. Modifying Figure 6.1 slightly you can see the relationship between capacity and the volume of services demanded (see Figure 6.2).

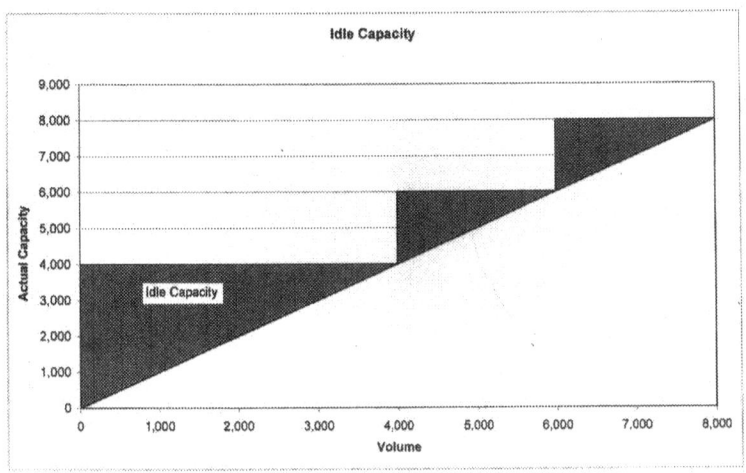

Figure 6.2

The shaded area represents the difference between the capacity of the machine (the step line) and the volume of services demanded (the straight line going diagonally up the chart). This difference is the excess or unused capacity for the machine. For example, if ABI has three machines running 5,000 items and their combined capacity is 6,000 items then there is an idle capacity of 1,000 items. This extra capacity can be used to process items from other areas, provide room for future growth or be used for maintenance and finding ways to improve the accuracy and efficiency of the machines.

Tip:

In most cases you don't want to be operating at capacity. One reason is that volumes naturally fluctuate. If you are operating at capacity, then there is no room to handle these periodic fluctuations. In addition, the idle capacity must be large enough to account for planned maintenance, unplanned repairs, training, vacations, etc. without impacting the services provided to the customer.

VARIABLE COSTS

Variable costs are those that vary with the volume of services demanded from a department. They increase as the volume increases and decrease as the volume decreases. For example: ABI is charged $15.00 for each credit check done on a new loan applicant. This charge would be considered a variable cost. The more applications submitted, the greater the total cost of credit checks. The costs move in tandem with the number of applications, as shown in Figure 6.3.

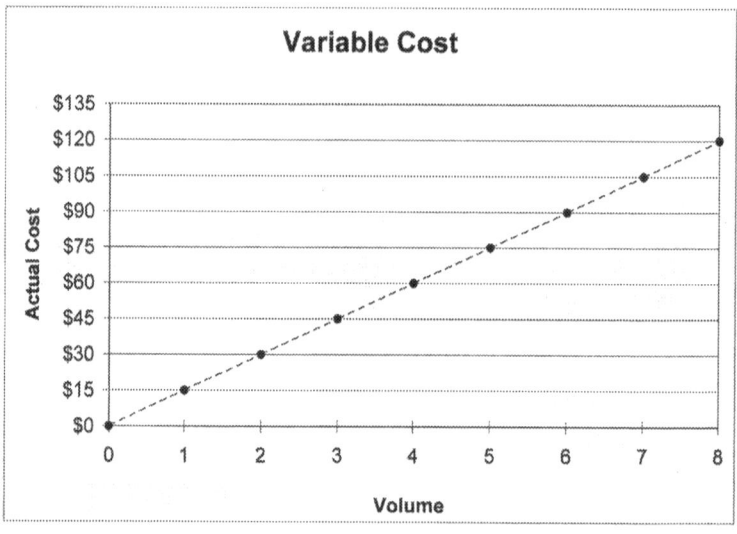

Figure 6.3

Figure 6.3 shows how the variable costs change in relation to the number of applications (volume). As the volume increases, the variable cost increases in lockstep with the volume by $15 per application. Since there is no difference between volume of credit checks performed and the volume paid for, there is no idle capacity.

SEMI-VARIABLE COSTS

Sometimes you will hear of a third classification of costs called semi-variable. It is usually a waste of time and serves no useful purpose. Semi-variable costs are those that people believe are in the grey areas. Items that are neither fixed nor variable. The thought is that some items are fixed for a certain period of time or volume and then variable thereafter.

There are several problems with this reasoning. First, all costs are variable in the long run. So, with the reasoning above you would have no fixed costs at all. Only variable and semi-variable. You are just trading one terminology for another.

Second, creating and maintaining semi-variable costs is non-value added work. If a cost varies with the volume then it is a variable cost. If it stays fixed for a period of time or within a certain range of volumes, then it is a fixed cost. If you want to show, figure and manage the idle capacity then it's a fixed cost. If not, then it is likely variable.

In short, don't waste time defining and justifying something that has no practical value. Remember, the top 90% of your costs will be obvious. The remainders are likely so small that they will have no impact on the overall ABC costs. The world won't end because a small item was chosen as one over another. Make your best guess (fixed or variable), then move on.

What are variable and fixed costs used for?

Variable and fixed costs are used in Product pricing and capacity management. For example, lets say a sales person at ABI is selling payment services to a new customer. The customer would add from 500 to 700 payments per month. The sales person would want to know two things:

1. What price should be charged?

2. Does ABI have the capacity to add 500 to 700 more items per month?

First, recall that your fixed costs determine your capacity. As the demand for your services increases, no additional fixed costs are added until you approach your capacity limit. However, variable costs increase in tandem with the volume of services demanded.

So, lets assume ABI is using the numbers in Figure 6.2. We know that ABI is currently processing 3,000 items per month and has the capacity of 4,000. Based on the graph, ABI has the capacity to add another 500 to 700 items before more capacity and fixed costs need to be added (question 2). Since, ABI can handle the increase in volume without adding more machines, no additional fixed costs will be incurred. Further, assuming the existing relationships are already covering all of the fixed costs, the minimum price that must be charged (question 1) is the variable cost. Pricing at any level above the variable cost will simply add more revenue to the bottom line.

If the existing relationships have not fully covered the fixed cost, then pricing above the variable cost is required to cover the fixed cost. Any price higher than the variable cost will cover more of the fixed cost than ABI is currently covering. All fixed costs must be covered in order for the service to break even or make a profit.

Remember, regardless of whether the new customer is added or not added, the company will still pay the same fixed costs for the same capacity of 4,000. It is a sunk cost. However, adding more volume to ABI will incrementally increase the variable costs. So, Sales Teams need to charge enough to cover the variable costs plus a little extra to contribute to the fixed cost or the bottom line.

How do you know if existing customers are already covering the fixed costs?

You can determine if your existing customers are already covering your fixed costs by looking at the Product Profitability Report. The Product Profitability Report compares the revenues generated to the total of the fixed costs, variable costs, idle capacity, and overhead costs. Obviously, the higher a Price the sales person can charge and still win the new business, the better. But, if the Product or service shown on the Product Profitability Report is already profitable, then all applicable costs are being covered. In which case, it is safe to price as low as the variable cost, if that's what it takes to win the bid. A more detailed breakeven analysis can also be done and will be explained later in this book.

Labor Costs—Fixed or Variable?

Exempt labor is considered a fixed cost because it doesn't fluctuate based on the volume or services demanded. Benefits for exempt personnel are usually included as fixed as well for the same reason. You can try to go line-by-line through the General Ledger to determine which benefits are fixed or variable costs. But that's a lot of work and you generally don't have much control over benefits anyway. The quickest way is to classify the benefits for exempt employees the same as exempt labor and the benefits for non-exempt the same as non-exempt labor.

Non-exempt labor (production labor) is usually classified as variable costs. However, this classification should be done with caution. In some organizations, labor is actually treated as fixed. For example, in the services industries, most of the non-exempt employees work a full eight hours regardless of the day-to-day volume fluctuations. This fact would lead one to believe that most of the salaries are fixed costs. Yet, managers desire to classify most of the labor as variable cost. Thus, classifying labor cost as fixed or variable must be considered carefully. Consider the Table 6.1 for each department when deciding if the non-exempt labor is a variable or fixed cost.

Rule of Thumb: Fixed/Variable Cost Classification

Table 6.1

Labor is considered a variable cost when...	Labor is considered a fixed cost when...
1. Non-overtime labor hours fluctuate from time to time depending on the volume fluctuations. (Note: Overtime is usually a variable cost).	1. Idle capacity reporting is desired.
2. Employees are sent home early (or offered the opportunity) when the work is complete.	2. Employees work the full eight hours each day.
3. Employees are loaned to other departments when their work is complete and their hours are similarly charged to the other department.	3. Employees generally work for the same department each and every day.
4. Employees who have finished their work, but choose to remain in their department for the remainder of the day have their time charged to non-Product related functions (i.e. maintenance, workstation clean-up, idle capacity, *etc.* which are categorized as fixed costs).	4. Employee hours are charged to the same job code for the entire day regardless of the amount of work completed.

Some people argue (often vehemently) that non-exempt/production labor should always be variable, but seldom understand why. They may say "that's the way its always been done, so it has to be that way". Whenever someone makes a statement like that, flashing red lights should go off in your head. Such statements are an opportunity for process improvement.

They are right from the standpoint that traditional (manufacturing) production labor is considered variable cost. But it is not necessarily true in the services industry. In manufacturing when a person performs a task on a Product, his time is charged to that function (variable cost). When all the work is complete, he begins work on another Product and charges his time to that Product/function (variable cost). If there is no more work, he is either sent home early (No Cost) or is offered the opportunity to finish his shift by performing plant maintenance. If he chooses to remain, the remainder of his shift is charged to maintenance (fixed cost). This fixed maintenance cost includes cleaning up the shop, preventative maintenance, *etc.* and must be approved by management. Thus, for manufacturing, time spent on Product related work is charged as variable and non-Product related work is charged (and closely managed) as fixed cost. Notice how this fits nicely with the questions in Table 6.1.

Now consider the services industry. Many employees work the full eight hours every day regardless of the volume fluctuations from one day to the next. The full eight hours of time is often charged to their department and hence the Product or service they support. When the employee is loaned to another area for one afternoon a week, their time is often charged incorrectly. It is normally kept in the original department and not charged to the adopted department. Consequently, the cost is not shown on the adopted department's Products. This understates the costs and overstates the profitability of the adopted department/Product.

Over time the services industry will become more competitive. As it does, servicing (production) labor will more closely reflect that of manufacturing. Until then, don't blindly follow conventional wisdom. Classify labor as a variable cost only if it is being used as a variable resource. Consciously examine your labor and classify it as fixed or variable based on the definitions in this book.

The last item to consider when classifying labor as fixed or variable is whether you want excess labor to be counted as idle capacity. Remember that variable costs by definition vary with the volume and <u>have no idle capacity</u>. Fixed costs do not vary with volume and do have excess or idle capacity. Examine your own situation using the questions and examples above to determine, department by department, what is fixed and what is variable. A sample list of fixed and variable costs is included Appendix B.

VARIABLE PRICING

Variable pricing is quoting the customer price based on variable cost, instead of the total service cost (fixed and variable). This technique is used by Sales teams to win bids on new business. Some people cringe at the thought of this. They worry that if all accounts were charged this way then the company would not make enough money to cover the fixed costs and add to the profitability. This is true, in theory. However, there are already systems in place that provide checks and balances for variable pricing.

First, recall the discussion on variable costs. If existing customers cover all the fixed costs, then pricing at anything above the variable cost is gravy. Second, sales teams are held accountable for profitability through their incentive plans. Most of the sales teams are rewarded based on the overall profitability of their customers. Profitability (revenues - total cost) is based on the total cost of the service (including fixed, variable, idle capacity, and overhead costs) not just the variable cost. So, when a sales person uses variable pricing, it is a very conscious decision. He must make certain he can make up the difference in fees or other services for the same customer. Otherwise, he'll risk losing his incentive and possibly his job for having an unprofitable portfolio of customer accounts.

Stakeholders are also indifferent as to which services for a particular customer are net losses. As long as the overall portfolio of accounts is profitable, stakeholders are happy. We will discuss more about the responsibilities of different areas and the checks and balances of the ABM system later. The important thing to remember is that the more the Sales Team can charge and still win the bid, the better off everyone will be. And at times, this may mean charging at or just above the variable cost, to win a bid.

ABC COSTING METHODS

There are two basic methods for calculating the ABC costs from the activity times. They are the Hourly Rate Method and the Resource Costing Method. The Hourly Rate Method is very popular and easy to use. However, it is also the less preferred of the two methods. The Resource Costing Method is just as easy, but is immensely more powerful for ABM. Both of these methods will be discussed below.

Hourly Rate Method

The Hourly Rate Method is the process of taking a department's total expenses and dividing by the total working hours to calculate an average cost per labor hour. This is often referred to as the hourly rate. The hourly rate (in dollars per hour) is then multiplied by the activity time (decimal hours per item) to get the ABC cost. Most companies will use the department's total expenses in the calculations. Using total expenses with all departments, allows you to "absorb" all the company's costs in the hourly rates.

For example, lets say Department B at ABI has $180,150 in expenses and an employee can process 50 items per hour. Assuming the department has 6 employees the hourly rate would be calculated as follows:

Department B Hourly Rate Calculation:

of Employees * Hrs/Wk * Wks/Year = Working Hours per Year

6 Employees * 40 Hrs per Wk * 52 Weeks per Year = 12,480 Working Hrs/Year

Hourly Rate = $180,150/12,480 Working Hours = $14.44 per Hour

Department B ABC Cost Calculation:

Multiply the hourly rate ($14.44) by the activity time 0.0200 hours (or 1 hour/50 items) and the ABC cost is $0.2887 per item.

Obviously, these are very simple calculations. There are also several variations and ways to fine-tune this method. One is to separate the costs into two categories: fixed and variable. Then divide the total fixed costs by the total working hours and total variable costs by the total working hours. This gives you fixed and variable hourly rates. You can then multiply each rate by the activity time for a given transaction to come up with the fixed and variable ABC costs. These calculations are shown below using Department B and its activity times from table 5.1.

Department B Fixed and Variable Hourly Rate Calculation:

6 Employees x 40 Hours per Week x 52 Weeks per Year = 12,480 Working Hours/Year

Total Fixed Expenses ($9,800)/12,480 Working Hours = $0.79/Hour
Total Variable Expenses ($170,350)/12,480 Working Hours = $13.65/Hour
Net Hourly Rate = Fixed Hourly Rate ($0.79) + Variable Hourly Rate ($13.65) = $14.44

Department B ABC Cost Calculation:

ABC Cost = Activity Time x Hourly Rate

Fixed ABC Cost = 0.0200 Hours * $0.79 per Hour = $0.0157
Variable ABC Cost = 0.0200 Hours * $13.65 per Hour = $0.2730
Total ABC Cost = Fixed UC ($0.0157) + Variable UC ($0.2730) = $0.2887

Thus, it costs $0.2887 each time an item is processed in Department B ($0.0157 fixed and $0.2730 variable). This method of ABC cost calculation is quick and easy. However, the Hourly Rate Method has two drawbacks:

1. The Hourly Rate Method provides little information for capacity management or process improvement.

2. The Hourly Rate Method does nothing to assist the manager in day-to-day operations.

For example, Department B at Average Business Incorporated processes three types of transactions with the following ABC costs and volumes.

Table 6.2

Cost Driver	Fix UC	Var UC	Vol	Fixed Cost	Variable Cost	Total ABC
Payments	$0.0200	$0.1800	105,000	$2,100	$18,900	$21,000
Transfers	$0.0100	$0.1900	256,000	$2,560	$48,640	$51,200
Close Account	$1.0000	$5.0000	1,300	$1,300	$6,500	$7,800
Total ABC Costs				$5,960	$74,040	$80,000

For Activity Based Management, the manager would compare his ABC costs with the actual expenses. The variance (difference) shows where there is room for improvement. It is where more money was actually spent (General Ledger expenses) than it should have cost (ABC cost) to provide the same number and mix of services. ABM using the Hourly Rate Method is shown below.

Table 6.3

	Fixed	Variable	Total
ABC Costs	$5,960	$74,040	$80,000
Actual Expenses	$9,800	$170,350	$180,150
Variance	$3,840	$96,310	$100,150

Table 6.3 is intended to show that Department B has an idle capacity. In this case, the total variance is $100,150. The variance is assumed to be idle capacity. But, this is not necessarily true. The variance could be caused by a number of things: 1) supplies ran considerably over for the time period, 2) new software was installed to resolve regulatory requirements, 3) there is some other cost that's higher than when the study was completed, *etc.*

Assuming it is idle capacity, what type is it? Is this idle labor, idle machines, unused occupancy, *etc.*? The Hourly Rate Method tells nothing about this. The Hourly Rate Method provides none of this information for you. It reveals little that an operations manager can utilize to run his day-to-day operations. Under the Hourly Rate Method, you'd need to go back and do comparisons of the study period expenses versus current expenses. The comparison would be tedious, slow, and painful.

Operations folks don't have time for such tail chasing. They want to see a quick report, make a decision, and take action. Well-designed ABM systems should give managers the power to know exactly which of the cost items are out of line with the ABC costs. This information enables them to make better decisions on how to adjust costs. Is this a one-time hit, or will it be a recurring expense? If it is recurring, they can seek out the Activity Based Management Team and recommend an update to the ABC costs.

The next problem is process improvement. Using the Hourly Rate Method, the manager at Department B does not know what makes up the costs or where the resources are being consumed. A well-designed ABM system shows this at a glance. The Resource Costing Method solves all these issues and, thus, has become the preferred method for Activity Based Management Teams.

Adjusting for Vacations, Holidays and Sick Days:

It is possible to fine-tune the Hourly Rate Method one step further. The fine-tuning is done by adjusting for vacations, holidays, and sick days in the hourly rates calculation. The adjustment is made with the intent to make the hourly rates more accurate. Below is an example of how ABI could use this for ABC calculations.

Total Working Hours per Year = 52 weeks * 40 hours per week = 2,080 Working Hours

Working Hours:	2,080
Less Vacation (2 weeks x 40 hours per week):	-80

Less Holidays (8 x 8 hours per days):	-64
Less Sick Time (5 days x 8 hours per day):	-40
Total Operating Hours:	**1,896**

Then replace Working Hours with Operating Hours to calculate an hourly rate. The example below shows how this is calculated and the resulting ABC cost.

Fixed and Variable Hourly Rate Calculation:

6 Employees * 1,896 Hours per Year = 11,376 Operating Hours/Year

Total Fixed Expenses ($9,800)/11,376 Operating Hours = $0.86/Hour
Total Variable Expenses ($170,350)/11,376 Operating Hours = $14.97/Hour
Net Hourly Rate = Fixed Hourly Rate ($.86) + Variable Hourly Rate ($14.97) = $15.84

ABC Cost Calculation:

ABC Cost = Activity Time x Hourly Rate

Fixed ABC Cost = 0.0200 Hours * $0.86 per Hour = $0.0172
Variable ABC Cost = 0.0200 Hours * $14.97 per Hour = $0.2995
Total ABC Cost = Fixed UC ($0.0172) + Variable UC ($0.2995) = $0.3167

Compare this ABC cost using the Operating Hours ($0.3167) with the original one ($0.2887). This is a net increase of 10% in the ABC cost. It is a truer ABC cost, but will it really change any of your decisions? You'll probably find that people start debating what amounts to use for vacations, and personal time. Product Managers will want to show a lower number of days since it decreases the ABC costs thereby improving their Product profitability. Operations will want a larger amount of days because that would increase the ABC cost and make their ABC variances more favorable. Then people will want to add in training time, mandatory team meetings, *etc.* Before getting to conversations like this one, ask yourself, "What behaviors will this promote (good and bad)?" And "What value will the extra calculation add to the company?" Often you'll find this is a non-value added exercise.

Tip:

If you decide to go through this exercise, set some ground rules. Narrow it down to just the items ABI used in the examples above (Vacations, Holidays, and Sick/Personal Time). Then go to Human Resources to find out what the average is for your company as a whole and use those figures. While you are at it, find out from HR what the industry average is. This may be another item for you to look at when you are trying to improve productivity and decrease turnover.

Resource Costing Method

The Resource Costing Method is much more accurate, yet it is still easy to perform. With this method, you look at how your resources are utilized, and use that to calculate your ABC costs. Sometimes this is referred to as capacity costing. You use the same basic information as the Hourly Rate Method, but the result is significantly more powerful. Lets look at an example.

Initiate a Payment ABC Cost Resource Costing Calculation:

Basic Calculation: Cost per Resource * Amount of Resource Consumed

Assume:
Employees earn $10/hr.
Each payment takes 0.0200 Hours

Thus,
$10/Hour * 0.0200 Hours per payment = $0.2000/Payment Processed

So, each payment costs $0.2000 in processing labor. Again not rocket science; it is a straightforward calculation. This same calculation can be done across the remainder of the costing items (benefits, occupancy, equipment depreciation, *etc.*). You can do this manually, in a spreadsheet, or in a database to save yourself time. Spreadsheets and databases will make the process faster, more consistent, and repeatable. There are also many software packages available to do this. Such packages can save you the time of developing your own. You can use them to do all the calculations behind the scenes. The software packages also help you set up the results in a format designed specifically for reporting. Finally, you can use the software to run what-if scenarios, incorporate flow charts, *etc.* using the same information.

Tip:

Before you purchase an ABC/ABM software package, make sure you review Appendix E—Selecting an ABC Software Package. Following this simple example on software selection could save you a lot of work, and heartache.

For the purposes of this discussion, we'll look at the ABI example in the following table.

Resource Costing Table

Table 6.4

Expense Category	Fixed/ Variable	Annual Expense	Resource Capacity	Resource Unit of Measure	Cost per Unit of Resource
Labor	Variable	$124,800	12,480	Labor Hours	$10.00
Benefits	Variable	$41,600	12,480	Labor Hours	$3.33
Total Personnel:		**$166,400**			
Repairs & Support	Variable	$650	12,480	Support Hours	$0.05
Equipment Depreciation	Fixed	$3,800	37,440	Machine Hours	$0.10
Occupancy	Fixed	$5,800	37,440	Occupancy Hours	$0.15
Total Property and Equipment:		**$10,250**			
Telecommunications	Variable	$1,100	12,480	Total Labor Hours	$0.09
Outside Services	Variable	$100	12,480	Total Labor Hours	$0.01

Table 6.4 (Continued)

Expense Category	Fixed/ Variable	Annual Expense	Resource Capacity	Resource Unit of Measure	Cost per Unit of Resource
Legal & Professional	Fixed	$200	12,480	Total Labor Hours	$0.02
Transportation	Variable	$1,200	12,480	Total Labor Hours	$0.10
Printing & Supplies	Variable	$900	12,480	Total Labor Hours	$0.07
Total Other Expenses:		$3,500			
Total Expenses:		$180,150			

It may look strange that there are only 12,480 total hours of capacity for labor, but that there are over 37,440 hours of capacity for the equipment depreciation and occupancy. The reason is that the machines are physically available (actual capacity) 24 hours a day (12,480 per shift x 3 shifts). It is acceptable to use 12,480 here instead, if you want to fully absorb the cost. However, you will want to know actual capacity of the machines for capacity management. This will be discussed more the Take Action section.

You may also notice that ABI used the total labor hours for the telecom and other expenses. This was done for expediency. You may want to know the exact cost per item for the "other expenses" in some areas. For example, you may want to use the actual cost per application for retrieving Credit Reports. This is typically a known cost (say $15 or $20 per Credit Report) and can be included as such. However, in Department B the "other expenses" are not easily itemized. The other expenses also account for just 2.5% of the department's total expenses and you'll rarely want to find the idle capacity for such a small item. So, the costs, in this case, are spread over the total labor hours.

The next step is to multiply the cost of the resource by the amount of resources used per item processed. For example, based on the time study the department requires 0.0200 hours to process each item. This time or resource utilization rate (hours used per item) is multiplied by the cost per unit of resource. The result is the ABC cost contributed by each resource (labor, equipment depreciation, occupancy, *etc.*). These calculations are summarized in the table below.

Table 6.5

Expense Category	Fixed/ Variable	Cost per Unit of Resource	Resources Required per Item	Resource Cost Contribution per Item
Labor	Variable	$10.00	0.0200	$0.2000
Benefits	Variable	$3.33	0.0200	$0.0667
Total Personnel:				**$0.2667**
Repairs & Support	Variable	$0.05	0.0200	$0.0010
Equipment Depreciation	Fixed	$0.10	0.0200	$0.0020
Occupancy	Fixed	$0.15	0.0200	$0.0031
Total Property and Equipment:				**$0.0062**
Telecommunications	Variable	$0.09	0.0200	$0.0018
Outside Services	Variable	$0.01	0.0200	$0.0002
Legal & Professional	Fixed	$0.02	0.0200	$0.0003
Transportation	Variable	$0.10	0.0200	$0.0019
Printing & Supplies	Variable	$0.07	0.0200	$0.0014
Total Other Expenses:				**$0.0056**
Total ABC Cost:				**$0.2784**

Therefore, each payment processed through Department B at ABI costs $0.2000 for labor, $0.0010 for repairs and support, $0.0020 for equipment depreciation, *etc.* The total ABC cost is $0.2784. Notice this cost is different from the Hourly Rate Method ($0.2887). The reason is that the Resource Costing Method uses several different divisors so we can do capacity management. The Hourly Rate Method only uses one divisor (operating hours). For example, the Hourly Rate Method assumed 12,480 hours across all resources. So, we could have substituted 12,480 hours for resource capacity on the equipment depreciation and occupancy to get an apple-to-apple comparison. This substitution would have given us the same result as the Hourly Rate Method ($0.2887).

As you can tell by the ABI examples, both of the calculations are very easy. So why go through a little extra effort and detail? The reason is that the Resource Costing Method provides you the ability to 1) monitor and improve capacity utilization, 2) maintain ABC costs, and 3) forecast costs for planning and budgeting. The first two will be shown in the next couple of steps. Forecasting and budgeting will be covered in the Take Action section (see Activity Based Budgeting and Planning—ABB/P).

The next step in Resource Costing is to take the ABC costs and multiply by the volumes each period. This calculation is fairly simple. In Department B, the ABM Team will multiply the labor contribution ($0.2000) by the number of payments processed (105,000 for the month). The result is a total ABC cost of $21,000 for labor. Continuing the process for the other expense items, the team gets the result shown below.

Table 6.6

Expense Category	Resource Cost Contribution per Item	Payment Volume	ABC Cost
Labor	$0.2000	105,000	$21,000
Benefits	$0.0667	105,000	$7,000
Total Personnel:	**$0.2667**	**105,000**	**$28,000**
Repairs & Support	$0.0010	105,000	$109
Equipment Depreciation	$0.0020	105,000	$213
Occupancy	$0.0031	105,000	$325
Total Property and Equipment:	**$0.0062**	**105,000**	**$648**
Telecommunications	$0.0018	105,000	$185
Outside Services	$0.0002	105,000	$17
Legal & Professional	$0.0003	105,000	$34
Transportation	$0.0019	105,000	$202
Printing & Supplies	$0.0014	105,000	$151
Total Other Expenses:	**$0.0056**	**105,000**	**$589**
Total:	**$0.2784**	**105,000**	**$29,237**

Next, roll these costs up by department and compare the ABC costs to the Actual expenses. This roll-up results in something similar to a variance report. A sample variance report for the Department B is shown below.

Table 6.7

Expense Category	Fixed/ Variable	Actual Expense	Activity Based Cost	Variance ($)	Variance (%)
Labor	Variable	$124,800	$100,000	$24,800	24.80%
Benefits	Variable	$41,600	$33,000	$8,600	26.06%
Total Personnel:		**$166,400**	**$133,000**	**$33,400**	**25.11%**
Repairs & Support	Variable	$650	$700	($50)	-7.14%
Equipment Depreciation	Fixed	$3,800	$3,700	$100	2.70%
Occupancy	Fixed	$5,800	$5,550	$250	4.50%
Total Property and Equipment:		**$10,250**	**$9,950**	**$300**	**3.02%**
Telecommunications	Variable	$1,100	$900	$200	22.22%
Outside Services	Variable	$100	$75	$25	33.33%
Legal & Professional	Fixed	$200	$150	$50	33.33%
Transportation	Variable	$1,200	$900	$300	33.33%
Printing & Supplies	Variable	$900	$800	$100	12.50%
Total Other Expenses:		**$3,500**	**$2,825**	**$675**	**23.89%**
Total Expenses:		**$180,150**	**$145,775**	**$34,375**	**23.58%**

The variance report is the most common Activity Based Management view used by Operations Managers. This report is also the one people think of most when they talk about ABM. The actual expense is what the department manager physically paid for the different expense lines. The Activity Based Cost shows what it should have cost given the same mix and volume of services demanded.

Compare Table 6.7 to the report using the Hourly Rate Method in Table 6.3. Do you see how powerful the Resource Costing Method is? You can tell that the department spent 25% more on labor and 7% less on repairs and support than it should have according to the ABC costs. Assuming the ABC costs are up to date, this means that there is 25% idle capacity in labor. The analysis also tells the manager that the occupancy and equipment were near capacity. As a result, the manager at Department B will also be monitoring the Equipment variance closely (which appears to be at capacity). If the Repairs and Support continue to be lower than the ABC then he may also recommend that the ABC costs be updated.

You can examine each of the other lines and compare them to prior time-periods. Comparisons across periods help identify long-term trends. Based on the trends you can make some decisions about costs, pricing, and management of the department. This is the heart of Activity Based Management.

It is important to keep the ABC costs accurate and up-to-date because that is what the Sales team uses to set prices and the managers use to manage. You can quickly analyze the report to find opportunities for improvement, which items need to be managed better, and whether the ABC costs need to be updated. If ABC costs need updating, it is often not necessary to do a whole new study. Just update the particular expense category that has changed (*i.e.* repairs and support). Don't worry about including the idle capacity in the ABC costs. That will be handled later when calculating the total service cost (which is used for profitability reporting).

Tip:

Appendix F—Common Causes of ABC Variance contains a quick list of some common symptoms and possible causes of variance in your ABM reports.

How to handle departments with both salaried and hourly employees

Some departments have both salaried and hourly employees. You have several alternatives in these areas:

1. Keep the resource costs and activity times separate. This is the preferred action since it differentiates between fixed and variable costs. Simply, create one line for salaried labor and one line for hourly labor. The cost per unit of resource ($ per hour) for each is then multiplied by its

resource utilization rate (i.e. activity times). Remember that the fixed and variable costs will be added together when calculating the total ABC cost of each transaction. Likewise for the activity times. You must consider that when figuring the activity times, otherwise you will be doubling the cost.

2. Lump the salaries together to come up with an aggregated resource cost for all employees in the department. Then calculate the ABC cost normally. This technique is quick, but it skews capacity management since fixed and variable costs are now mixed together.

3. Break the transaction into separate Cost Drivers. For example, you may want to do this when salaried employees work mainly on problem transactions, or problem accounts. If that occurs regularly, then you may want to track the cost separately under a separate Cost Driver.

How to handle Vendor Costs

Items listed in "other expenses" are sometimes incurred through vendors. These vendors often charge based on the number of transactions. The vendor costs are thus considered variable costs. A good example is Credit Reports for processing a loan application. Companies usually pay a third party vendor to perform this function. It is usually a nominal fee per credit check. In such cases, you can figure out the resource costing as shown Table 6.8.

Table 6.8

Expense Category	Fixed/ Variable	Cost per Unit of Resource	Resources Required per Item	Resource Cost Contribution per Item
Credit Reports	Variable	$15.00	1	$15.00

This item is appended to the bottom of the Resource Costing Table (Table 6.5). Then you can continue the Resource Costing Method normally. Be sure you don't double count the costs. If you use an amount for vendor costs, make sure that amount is not included in the other amounts in Table 6.4. This could save you a lot of headaches later on.

Tip:

The Vendor Costs approach can be used for internal vendors or subsidiaries. The only difference is that the money just moves from one spot to another on paper.

Tip:

The Vendor Costs approach can be used if you know that a specific amount of floor space in a department is dedicated to a particular service or function. Simply figure out what portion of the department's total square feet it is, then multiply that by the total occupancy expense, and continue the calculations as shown in Tables 6.4–6.6. The only difference is you'd now have two occupancy lines.

How to handle costs for Call Centers and Telemarketing areas

There are several unique costs associated with Call Centers (inbound) and Telemarketing areas (outbound). Labor, occupancy, and some equipment costs can be handled using standard Resource Costing. However, the telecommunication costs for these areas need special consideration.

In telecom centric areas, you need to evaluate which parts of the telecom costs are fixed and which are variable. For example, if you pay a fee for a certain amount of dedicated lines regardless of their usage then the costs would be fixed. Fixed telecom costs can be calculated similar to the occupancy cost under standard Resource Costing. Make sure your the resource capacity takes into account the number of lines available, hours available (24/7/365) *etc.* If you have a pay per usage (i.e. cost per minute) plan, then the costs would be variable. Variable costs can be handled using the "Vendor Costs" methodology used for Credit Reports or through time studies like those done for the labor component.

How to handle costs for Mail Operations

Mail Operations departments need special consideration for their postage, supply, equipment, and transportation costs. These costs should be broken out on a per item basis whenever possible. The per item costs are variable and can be treated similar to the "Vendor Costs" methodology used for Credit Reports. Equipment costs can be calculated similar to the equipment and depreciation costs.

How to study Information Systems and Technology areas

Another advantage of using the Resource Costing Method is that it can be adapted for Information Systems and Technology areas. In fact, Resource Costing is ideal for calculating systems support and machine utilization. As shown in Table 6.4, you can use machine hours to calculate the resource cost per machine hour, then the cost per item.

You can also break utility and technology items into more detail. In this case, ABI adds a column called "Costing Category". This extra information allows ABI to break telecom into two separate lines for costing. The first category is for the T1 high-speed connection. The T1 is a fixed cost by nature because the company pays the same cost each time regardless of how much this pipeline is used. The second category is for Long-Distance/Dial-Up access. This is used as a back up for the T1, so the company normally pays by the number of minutes utilized. Thus, Long-Distance is a variable cost. Tables 6.9 and 6.10 show an example of calculating the ABC cost using Resource Costing with Information Systems and Technology Areas.

Table 6.9

Expense Category	Costing Category	Fixed/ Variable	Annual Expense	Resource Capacity (Annual)	Resource Unit of Measure	Cost per Unit of Resource
Labor	Labor	Fixed	$62,400	2,080	Labor Hours	$30.00
Equipment Depreciation	ATM Transaction Processing System	Fixed	$3,000	6,000	Machine Hours	$0.50
Telecom	T-1 Line	Fixed	$837	18.6	MB	$45.00
Telecom	Long-Distance/ Dial-Up	Variable	$500	6,000	Minutes	$0.08
Outside Services	Third Party (Off-Site) Data Backup	Variable	$60,000	1,200,000	MB of Storage	$0.05

Table 6.10

Expense Category	Costing Category	Fixed/ Variable	Cost per Unit of Resource	Resources Required per Item	Resource Cost Contribution per Item
Labor	Labor	Fixed	$30.00	0.00012	$0.0036
Equipment Depreciation	ATM Transaction Processing System	Fixed	$0.50	0.00015	$0.0001
Telecom	T-1 Line	Fixed	$45.00	0.0001	$0.0045
Telecom	Long-Distance/Dial-Up	Variable	$0.08	0.1	$0.0083
Outside Services	Third Party (Off-Site) Data Backup	Variable	$0.05	0.002	$0.0001

You may not need the "Costing Category" column in your system, but it helps to ensure the clarity of the information. Also, notice how all the calculations are the same as those in the rest of Resource Costing. The resource capacities reflect the annualized capacity of the resource. For example, lets say ABI is charged by an outside vendor $50 per Gigabyte of storage each period and ABI Corporation normally measures capacity in Megabytes. This means that if the company wants to have 100 GB (100,000 MB) of off site data storage capacity each period, then the annual capacity is 1,200,000 MB (100,000 MB x 12 Months). The same type of calculation was done for the T-1 line capacity (1.55 MB/sec x 12 Months).

There are several variations on this method depending on the volume and statistics available:

Variation 1: Let's say you want to calculate the cost based on the amount of server space the systems utilize. First, you need to know the amount of storage available on a given server (capacity) and roughly how much of the resource each transaction or service consumes. Use these statistics as the resource capacity on Table 6.9 and the resources required on Table 6.10. This allows you to come up with a good method for costing the services. Then on a recurring basis (or for each reporting period) you load the new usage statistics in as a volume.

<u>Variation 2:</u> Lets say you want to calculate the cost of a service based on the amount of system processing time utilized (i.e. for month end reporting or statement cycle processing). This can be done if you know the planned up time (capacity) for the system and the actual usage time required (resources required per item). You can then develop the ABC costs for the services as shown above.

<u>Variation 3:</u> Lets say you want to create costs for programmers and new systems development. Programmers can be costed based on their working hours (2,080) and the amount of time they spend supporting a particular platform or process. New systems development work (Research and Development) and platform support are not usually included in ABC costs. Instead, new systems development should be tracked as a separate project and depreciated with along with the equipment during its expected useful life. Your accounting staff can often help you with this task. Software development efforts can also be tracked and compared to the planned/budgeted Capital Expenditures for the effort. This type of analysis will help you plan more successfully for future projects. Platform support is often shared between systems and is included with the SG&A costs. SG&A will be discussed later in the book.

INCLUDING IDLE CAPACITY AND SG&A FOR PROFITABILITY

We haven't discussed idle capacity and SG&A costs up to this point. The reason is that idle capacity and SG&A are not processing costs and therefore are not included in the ABC costs. Yet, they are costs that need to be managed. ABM is an excellent tool for this as well. For example, managers are held accountable for minimizing idle capacity through variance reporting. They are held accountable for keeping their expenses in line (or within an acceptable range) with their ABC costs. This can be done both in total and by resource using Resource Costing. Achieving this range will, by design, keep the idle capacity under control. Thus, idle capacity is identified because of ABC, <u>not</u> as a part of ABC.

However, the idle capacity and SG&A (or overhead departments) costs must be included in the total service cost for profitability reporting. Showing these items on Product and Customer Profitability Reports highlights the fact that there is idle capacity and that there is an overhead cost involved in the running a business. Using total service cost (ABC + idle capacity + SG&A) causes Sales and Administrative managers to improve their own areas as well as supporting improvements in operations. Another benefit of using total service cost for profitability is that it keeps Operations and Business Unit folks from hiding expenses in administrative departments where ABC and ABM may not be as tightly controlled. These are just a few examples of the Checks and Balances that make ABM so powerful. Idle capacity and SG&A are discussed in more detailed below.

Idle Capacity

Idle capacity is simply the difference between the total ABC cost and the Total actual expenses. Idle capacity is also known as unused capacity or excess capacity. Generally what you call it depends on how politically correct you want to be. Idle capacity is managed through ABC Variance Reports at the department level. However, it can be very difficult to calculate the idle capacity cost at every level and for every Product or Service. You also don't want it changing every month on profitability reports since constant cost fluctuations create a moving target for the Sales force. Instead, it is best if you come up with an aggregate for the corporation as a whole or by Business Unit.

You can get a reasonable estimate by looking at the previous year's ABC results. You simply look at the total variance between last year's ABC costs and the actual expenses. This variance can be used as an idle capacity estimate for the current year's profitability reports.

Tip:

If you don't have last year's results (because you are just starting ABM) try to reverse engineer it. Simply calculate last year's total ABC costs by using current ABC costs multiplied by last year's volumes. Then compare this with last year's expenses as shown above.

Tip:

As a last resort, if you can't do any of the items above, start with a rule of thumb of 15%. Then update using actual numbers after monitoring the system for a couple of months.

Calculating Idle Capacity %

Idle capacity is simply the difference between what it actually costs to process transactions (actual expenses) and what it should have cost (ABC costs). So, the idle capacity is actual expense minus total ABC cost. This sounds easy enough, so let us look at an example from ABI. We'll assume that ABI had $30,000,000 in actual expenses and $25,500,000 in total ABC cost last year. Based on this, the idle capacity dollars would be calculated as:

Idle Capacity Cost   = Actual Expense - Total ABC Cost
                                     = $30,000,000 - $25,500,000
                                     = $4,500,000

The idle capacity % is the percent expenses that are not utilized. Therefore, calculating the idle capacity % you simply divide the idle capacity cost by the actual expenses. In this case, you would see that ABI has an idle capacity of 15%.

The idle capacity rate is the tax or additional cost burden that will be added to the ABC cost to account for the idle capacity in profitability reports. This can be calculated in one of two ways.

The first technique for calculating an idle capacity rate is to look at the idle capacity dollars as a percent of the total ABC costs. Simply divide the idle capacity dollars by the total ABC costs. From the example above, the idle capacity rate can be calculated as:

Idle Capacity Rate   = Idle Capacity $/Total ABC Costs * 100
                                     = $4,500,000/$25,500,000 * 100
                                     = 17.6%

So the cost of each service will be taxed an additional 17.6% when calculating profitability. The second technique of calculating the idle capacity rate is just as simple. You simply divide one by (1 - idle capacity %). Using the numbers above, ABI's idle capacity rate would be calculated as:

Idle Capacity Rate   = 1/(1 - Idle Capacity %)
                                     = 1/(1 - 0.15)
                                     = 17.6%

Notice how this is the same result as the first calculation (17.6%). You can use either method, but we'll use the first method for the examples that follow. The important thing to remember is that the ABC costs will be increased by the idle capacity rate of 17.6% for profitability reporting. Do not use the idle capacity %

(15%). If you use the idle capacity %, you will be understating the true cost of running your business.

Applying Idle Capacity to ABC Cost

Lets assume that ABI performs only one type of function, originating loans. According to the time and cost studies, Loan Origination has an ABC cost of $90.00, a volume of 1,000, and their actual expenses were $106,200. ABI now wants to account for the idle capacity of the corporation in the cost portion of their profitability reports. The basic calculation for adjusting the ABC costs to include idle capacity is shown below.

Idle Capacity $	= Expenses - Total ABC Cost
	= $106,200 - ($90.00 * 1,000) = $16,200
Idle Capacity Rate	= Idle Capacity $/Total ABC Cost
	= $16,200/($90.00 * 1,000) *100% = 18.00%
Adjusted ABC Cost	= ABC Cost + (ABC Cost * Idle Capacity Rate)
	= $90.00 +($90.00 * 18.00%) = $106.20

Checking this result is straight forward, but requires a little math.

First recall:

1. Idle Capacity $ = Actual Expense - Total ABC Cost.

2. Total ABC Cost = Volume * ABC Cost

3. Idle Capacity $ = Idle Capacity Rate * Volume * ABC Cost

4. Adjusted ABC Cost = ABC Cost + (ABC Cost * Idle Capacity Rate)

Second, rearrange equation 1 to solve for actual expense:

5. Actual Expense = Total ABC Cost + Idle Capacity $

Next, replace total ABC cost and idle capacity $ in equation 4 with the right side of equations 2 and 3 respectively:

6. Actual Expense = Total ABC Cost + Idle Capacity $

7. Actual Expense = (Volume * ABC Cost) + (Idle Capacity Rate * Volume * ABC Cost)

Fourth, simplify the equation by pulling out the volume:

8. Actual Expense = (ABC Cost + (ABC Cost * Idle Capacity Rate)) * Volume

Finally, substitute adjusted ABC cost (from equation 4):

9. Actual Expense = [ABC Cost + (ABC Cost * Idle Capacity Rate)] * Volume

10. Actual Expense = [Adjusted ABC Cost] * Volume

So, we should get an amount equal to the actual expense by including the idle capacity in our ABC cost, and multiplying by the volume. Lets see:

Actual Expense   = Adjusted ABC Cost x Volume
                  = $106.20 x 1,000
                  = $106,200

The result equals the total actual expense we started with. This is not the best way to show the calculation in profitability reporting. That would be very daunting and confusing. A simpler way to show the idle capacity % for profitability reporting is to put it in the reports themselves. An example of this is shown below.

Table 6.11

	Total ABC Cost	Idle Capacity 18% x ABC Cost	SG&A 18% x ABC Cost	Total Cost (TC)	Revenues (Rev)	Net Profit (Rev— TC)
Portfolio A	$90,000	$16,200	$16,200	$122,400	$347,400	$225,000

Table 6.11 is how idle capacity and SG&A are normally shown. This keeps the idle capacity and SG&A (overhead) costs in clear view of everyone. Including all three components (ABC, idle capacity, and SG&A) in the total cost motivates everyone to:

1. Improve the operational areas (ABC cost)

2. Manage the idle capacity (Idle Capacity cost)

3. Decrease overhead costs (SG&A Cost)

4. Improve Sales (Revenues)

In this example, every service across the organization will be increased by the same percentage (18%). This is similar to a tax. In fact, many people refer to it as a costing tax. If you do this across the board, you will be covering the entire cost of idle capacity based on the percentage you calculated.

Note that the actual idle capacity may fluctuate from one reporting period to another. The fixed percent we calculated above is just an estimate of the corporation as a whole. The tax is used for pricing and profitability. Since ABI will be using the Resource Costing and ABM methodologies outlined in this book, the idle capacity will undoubtedly decrease over the course of the year. If that were the case then ABI would be over-estimating their costs and under-estimating the profitability. This over-estimation would continue until the idle capacity and SG&A Rates are updated. Just remember to monitor this closely and watch the trends. If you see trends up or down across the entire company, update the percentage.

Finally, you will be doing this calculation across the board, so you don't want to do it manually. That would be a maintenance nightmare. Let your ABM system do the drudgery. The only input you need to provide is the expected idle capacity rate, and that should only change once or twice a year. Below are some commonly asked questions about idle capacity.

How frequently should idle capacity be updated?—Adjusting the idle capacity percentage should be done annually (or semi annually if your idle capacity is significantly decreasing). Updating more frequently will cause fluctuations in the total service cost and a moving target for the Sales Team. So, monitor it closely, but only update a few times a year. Once a year will normally suffice.

At what level should idle capacity be calculated?—Idle capacity is managed at the department level through ABC Variance Reporting. However, it isn't necessary to calculate it department by department for profitability. For profitability, calculate the average for the whole corporation or by Business Unit. Then use this same rate in all the reports. It will cut down on the calculations considerably without affecting the usefulness of the data.

What is an acceptable level of idle capacity?—The acceptable limit of idle capacity is discussed later in the idle capacity Management section of this book. A common range is 10-15%, but that can vary by company, industry, and Business Unit. One of the great benefits of Activity Based Management and the Resource Costing Methodology used in this book is that the idle capacity for most areas is self-managing. Department managers are held accountable for keeping their expenses in line with the ABC costs. This accountability, by its very nature, decreases and controls the idle capacity.

Is idle capacity a fixed or variable cost?—Both. By definition, all idle capacity is fixed cost because it is the remainder of your unused fixed resources. It might also be considered as a variable cost since it fluctuates inversely with the volumes, i.e. as the volume increase the amount of idle capacity decreases. So technically, it can be classified as either a fixed or variable cost.

What is the difference between Idle, Unused and Excess Capacity?—These three terms are generally used interchangeably. However, once your ABM system is in place and functioning smoothly you may find it useful to refine this part of your ABM world. Very few ABM systems are sophisticated enough to account for and report on the differences. However, if you are brave enough (or bold enough), the different types of capacity are defined as follows:

Used Capacity—This is the productive time when the machines are actually running and the employees working. Occasionally (*i.e.* with automated machines) you may know the exact hours it was utilized. Otherwise, the standard proxy used for this is your activity times (resource requirements) multiplied by the volume for a given time period. You want to maximize your used capacity (capacity utilization) as much as possible.

Idle Capacity—Time when machines, people or processes are awaiting work from another upstream operation or awaiting additional resources to complete a task. Idle capacity is wasted time and should be minimized through process improvements such as Bottleneck Analyses and Six Sigma. See the Take Action section for more information on these.

Unused Capacity—Often called reserve capacity. Unused capacity is time that is not currently needed, but reserved for future sales growth, Product Line expansions or normal volume fluctuations. There is generally a business need for unused capacity, but it should be re-evaluated quarterly. After two quarters of being listed as unused capacity, and not utilized, these wasted resources revert to excess capacity and should be eliminated.

Excess Capacity—True waste. Excess capacity is excess resources above the amount needed now or in the near future. This wasted time must be eliminated. Excess capacity can be eliminated through a variety of capacity cuts, attrition, job sharing, *etc.*

SG&A

SG&A is defined as Sales, General, and Administrative. This is the cost of all the overhead areas (Sales, Finance, Accounting, Internal Audit, *etc.*). These departments cannot be managed using traditional ABC techniques. For example, managing a Sales Department is much different than managing an operational area. In Sales, most of the work is non-repetitive and relationship oriented. It varies with each meeting and customer. The variety of work does not lend itself to management under Activity Based Costing. In contrast, all processes after the sale is made can be included in ABC. The processing of applications, underwriting, payments, withdrawals, *etc.* are repetitive and can be included in ABC.

Another difference is that a lot of Sales is fixed cost (lots of salaried labor, occupancy, and depreciation). In ABC, fixed costs have a capacity and should be managed to control idle capacity. However, there should never be idle capacity in Sales. Sales folks should always be selling and expanding their relationships. Thus, SG&A departments are completely different from the processing areas and cannot be managed through traditional ABC.

This is not say that there isn't room for process improvement in Sales. There is. Just don't try to manage them like an operational area. So how should they be managed? There are many options such as setting budget targets, sales goals, customer profitability, incentives, key ratios, portfolio growth, *etc*. What gets measured and rewarded gets done. In Sales departments, this is usually accomplished through bonuses. The greater the profitability of a sales person's customer portfolio, the greater the bonus. This is fine, since the total service cost used for profitability includes ABC, idle capacity, and SG&A costs. It is to their advantage to both increase their revenues and decrease their portion (SG&A) of the total costs.

Calculating SG&A

The principle calculation of SG&A cost is analogous to the idle capacity calculation. Figure out what percent of the total corporation's cost is directly related to SG&A and add it to the ABC cost in the same manner as idle capacity. The result is an ABC cost breakdown like the one shown below (assuming Idle Capacity and SG&A rates of 15%).

Originate a Loan Process	*ABC Cost*
Sub-Driver: Complete Application	$25.75
Sub-Driver: Mail to Loan Operations	$1.50

Originate a Loan Process	ABC Cost
Sub-Driver: Process Application	$2.25
Sub-Driver: Underwriter Approval	$6.75
Sub-Driver: Mail back to Branch	$1.50
Sub-Driver: Book Loan	$50.75
Sub-Driver: Mail to Loan Operations	$1.50
Subtotal: Originate a Loan	**$90.00**
Sub-Driver: Idle Capacity (15% x $90.00)	$13.50
Sub Driver: SG&A (15% x $90.00)	$13.50
Total: Originate a Loan	**$117.00**

Tip:

To ensure accurate results, use the raw ABC cost for the calculation, not the adjusted ABC cost (including idle capacity).

Well there you have it. The total cost to Originate a Loan at ABI. This is the cost used for Product profitability, customer profitability, portfolio profitability, sales incentives, *etc.* You can break it out by fixed and variable cost as well, but for simplicity, we just showed the total here. Also, remember that just because the idle capacity says 15% on this report doesn't mean ALL departments have 15%. It is just an average. Some departments will have more, some will have less, but very few departments will have exactly 15%. For more ideas on how to improve SG&A or idle capacity, see the Take Action section later in this book. Below are a couple of Frequently Asked Questions about SG&A.

Can SG&A be subdivided into different categories? Yes, it can. Some organizations divide SG&A and overheads into several categories. These include Human Resources, Finance/Accounting, Audit, Information Technology and Business Unit (Sales and Business Unit Executives). You can then use a separate percentage for each. This technique can get a little more complicated. So it is best to start with just the one SG&A percent, then refine it to make the system more robust later. The benefit of the extra detail is that people start taking more ownership for their contribution to customer and Product profitability. Each organization should be held accountable for decreasing their costs and thereby their percentage cost contribution year over year.

Is SG&A a fixed or variable cost? SG&A can go either way and spending too much time on classifying it is non-Value-Added. But people generally think of it one of two ways. 1) By line item—all variable costs within SG&A departments are variable and all fixed costs within SG&A departments are fixed; or 2) As fixed cost since these departments are sunk costs that will remain with the company regardless of volume fluctuations until an improvement is made. The latter is simpler, faster, and its assumptions do not detract from the usability of the data nor the conclusions that you derive from them.

Step Seven: Summarize/Roll-Up Costs

Rolling up the costs is simply a matter of taking all the ABC Data you've collected, adding in the idle capacity and SG&A, then loading them into your ABM System. Often your ABM System will be housed within an existing Management Reporting system, Management Information System (MIS), Enterprise Resource Program (ERP), or Business Intelligence system. These systems may already contain much of the financial, organizational, and cost information needed for ABM. So centralizing the information prevents a duplication of effort in collecting and calculating the information. From the ABM perspective, the system should do a number of things:

1. Match the ABC costs with the volumes for each department for operational reporting (ABM).

2. Match the total service cost (ABC + idle capacity + SG&A) with the volumes for each Product and Cost Driver to calculate customer transaction profitability.

3. Summarize customer transaction profitability by customer for Portfolio Profitability.

4. Summarize customer transaction profitability by Product for Product and Business Unit profitability.

Finally, remember that operational managers use the ABC cost to monitor and improve their operational areas. Total service cost (including ABC, idle capacity, and SG&A) is used for Product, portfolio, Business Unit, and customer profitability. Below are a few common sticking points.

Frequency of Calculation

Rolling up the costs and running them through the ABM system usually occurs on a scheduled basis. Before you decide on the frequency, do a little research.

Many areas use cost and profitability numbers for monthly or quarterly incentives. In other instances, the information may be used in weekly or monthly reports prepared for executive management. So, make sure you can provide accurate costs on a consistent basis that coincides with the reporting needs above.

How often should the costs be updated?

This is like asking how often should inventory be counted in a warehouse to ensure it is correct. It should always be correct! Using the ABM methodology presented in this book, you will be continuously monitoring, updating, and improving the information. If you find an error or notice a trend on a report, research it, fix it, and move on. It should not be a once a year activity and it should not take a large amount of time. The techniques presented in this book enable you to update the information quickly and spend more time on process improvements than on analyses. Once the system is set up, the majority of the time should be spent on process improvements and estimating new costs.

Some corporations update their costs annually by throwing in the new budgeted expenses and recalculating all the costs. This process is often unnecessary since the costs in ABM are continually updated and refined. Updating the costs with budgeted amounts should only be used as a validation technique for the budget. Budget validation is covered in the ABB/P section later in this book.

HANDLING VARIANCES

What if there is a variance between the total actual expenses of the corporation and the total costs?

The Operations and Activity Based Management Teams should be monitoring the variances regularly and looking for trends. Differences (variances) can occur for a number of reasons. When operational expenses are higher than the total of the ABC and idle capacity cost then the corporation will have a variance. This trend might signal an increase in idle capacity. If so, you can adjust the idle capacity percent used in profitability reporting.

If expenses and costs are moving closer together then you might have decreasing idle capacity. A decrease in idle capacity may signal a need to update costs or highlight an area for improvement. Whichever the case, track down the root cause and perform improvements to fix the situation. Just make sure you communicate the information, especially if you can trace it to one particular Business Unit. There are no secrets in ABM

A change in SG&A expenses would also cause a variance. Like the idle capacity, the Activity Based Management Team should be looking for trends in SG&A expense. Then trace the root cause, and try to improve the area if possible. Meanwhile adjust the SG&A percent only when necessary and communicate this information.

Should the variance be allocated out?

No. ABM is not an allocation device. It should not be used as a balancing tool. The goal of ABM is to identify and report on the costs. You want to report the costs in a format that helps leaders to take action and make decisions.

The ABM and profitability methods presented in this book will be close to the actual expense, but will not tie exactly. If the costs are not close, the difference should be researched and action taken. Arbitrarily allocating the difference out does no good. It just sweeps the problem under the carpet and creates a lack of ownership. Either the costs need to be updated or the processes/business areas need to be improved. The fact that you recognize there is a problem means ABM is doing its job. Do not turn ABM into an Accounting or Allocations method.

How long should it take to validate ABM each reporting period?

It should only take an hour or two to validate ABM each reporting period. The review involves looking at the reports, highlighting the problem areas, and reprioritizing the project priority list. If the team spends more time than that on validation, then the system is too complicated or needs better automation. ABM isn't rocket science and the calculations should be done automatically within the system.

If an error is found during the validation, research, and fix it the core data. The core data is the actual cost study data, or the system that supplies the volumes. If you don't fix it at the source, the error will continue to plaque the system and confidence in ABM will suffer. Fix it right the first time. The majority of the ABM Team's time should be spent improving the operational processes and company profitability. ABM is about Taking Action.

USING THE SYSTEM

AKA: How to use ABM to generate profitability reports and Activity Based Management Team Reports.

You have already seen several of the reports that can be used in the ABM system. We'll review these and several others in more detail here. Standardized reports, such as the one's discussed in this book, are developed to increase the usability and timeliness of the ABM information. These reports are critical to the success of the company and the ABM system.

Unfortunately, reports are one area where people fail to think ahead. You need to consider the user's perspective when designing systems and reports. You need to know what they want to see and how they'll use the information. A lack of focus in design can waste a lot of time through rework. Poor report design can lead to misinformation and poor decision making by executives. Consequently, it makes sense to walk through several of the basic reports you'll need in this section.

Each report is used by different groups of people for different purposes. But it is all based on the same core ABC cost information. Information that was developed through the original ABC time study and Resource Costing. The information is simply rolled up and summarized at different levels depending on what you want to compare it to and what the users want to see. This means the same information is being seen from multiple viewpoints, which is a huge benefit of ABM. It provides ample opportunity for review, validation and improvement of the information. The reports can also be designed for users to dig or drill into for more detail, if that's desired. The reports below illustrate this and provide a good starting point for using the ABM system.

REPORTING

Product and servicing costs can be used for both the management of operations (as discussed previously), and customer/Product profitability. This section will discuss standard reports used in both situations. We'll start with a look at customer profitability reports typically used by Sales Teams. To develop this report it helps to begin with the raw transactional data that is used as a basis for all the reports.

Transaction Profitability

Transaction profitability is the lowest level of profitability reports and is used as a basis for all the others. Sometimes it is not even a report, but rather a table stored in the Management Information System. A table that acts as the data source for all the other profitability reports. Table 7.1 shows a sample Transaction Profitability Report from ABI.

Transaction Profitability Report

Table 7.1

Customer	Product	Cost Driver	Reve nue (Rev)	Total Service Cost	Vol um e	Total Cost (TC)	Profit (Rev— TC)
Customer A	Installment Loan # 1234	Origi- nate a Loan	$250	$117.00	1	$117.00	$133.00
Customer A	Installment Loan # 1234	Account Support	$50	$15.00	3	$45.00	$5.00
Customer A	Installment Loan # 1234	Initiate a Pay- ment	$0	$0.28	1	$0.28	($0.28)
Customer B	Installment Loan # 12345	Origi- nate a Loan	$250	$117.00	1	$117.00	$133.00
Customer B	Installment Loan # 12345	Account Support	$50	$15.00	3	$45.00	$5.00
Customer B	Demand Deposit # 123456	Account Support	$60	$3.75	2	$7.50	$52.50
Customer B	Installment Loan # 12345	Initiate a Pay- ment	$0	$0.28	4	$1.11	($1.11)

Note: Revenue is shown in aggregate for the purposes of this book. In reality, it may be made up of one or more components such as one-time fees (loan origination, appraisal etc.), recurring service charges, interest, transaction fees, and service fees *etc*. Also, note that the total cost (TC) includes ABC, idle capacity, and SG&A as discussed previously.

Table 7.1 shows that some customers have several accounts. In this case, Customer B has an Installment Loan and a Checking Account. Others might have a Savings Account, a Safe Deposit Box, and a Certificate of Deposit. Each account will have a separate account number and can be analyzed for profitability by account, customer or Product.

You probably won't use the Transaction Profitability Report (table) itself. Its main purpose is to accumulate the information needed to supply the other reports. For example, summarizing the accounts by customer gives the Customer Profitability Report (Customer A versus Customer B). Summarizing this same information by Product yields the Product Profitability Report (Checking versus Savings, Safe Deposit, and CD). Summarizing by customer portfolio results in the Portfolio Profitability Report (Portfolio A versus Portfolio B). Each of these reports will be discussed in turn and all the cost information can be linked directly back to ABM, idle capacity, and SG&A.

Customer Profitability

Sales Teams are the primary audience for the customer profitability reports. They use the report to monitor profitability and look for opportunities to improve the bottom line. Sales Executives, for example, may analyze the profitability of a customer and identify cross sell opportunities to improve the customer profit margins.

The reports are calculated by summarizing the transaction profitability information by customer or customer relationship. Sometimes the summarization by customer relationship is known as house holding, since it contains all accounts or customers related to the master customer account (or household). Table 7.2 summarizes the information from the Transaction Profitability Report by customer.

Customer Profitability Report

Table 7.2

Customer A

Product	Cost Driver	Revenues	Total Cost	Profit $	Profit %
Installment Loan	Originate a Loan	$250.00	$117.00	$133.00	53%
Installment Loan	Account Support	$50.00	$45.00	$5.00	10%
Installment Loan	Initiate a Payment	$0.00	$0.28	($0.28)	0%
	Total:	$300.00	$162.28	$137.72	46%

Customer B

Product	Cost Driver	Revenues	Total Cost	Profit $	Profit %
Installment Loan	Originate a Loan	$250.00	$117.00	$133.00	53%
Installment Loan	Account Support	$50.00	$45.00	$5.00	10%
Demand Deposit	Account Support	$60.00	$7.50	$52.50	88%
Installment Loan	Initiate a Payment	$0.00	$1.11	($1.11)	0%
	Total:	$360.00	$170.61	$189.39	53%

Table 7.2 shows the difference between the two customers and which Product Lines are profitable for which customers. From this simple analysis, the Sales Executive can see that the main difference is that Customer B has a Demand Deposit account, which has an 88% profit. In analyzing this further the Sales Executive realizes that its not just the Demand Deposit account, but all the ancillary service charges and fees that make the Demand Deposit so profitable. Noticing these items on several customers, the Sales Executive decides to cross-sell other customers (Customer A) to Demand Deposit to maximize his bonus.

ABM Teams use the Customer Profitability Report to see which customers are the least profitable. Then they brainstorm ideas with the Marketing and Sales teams to improve the profitability or target future Sales efforts at the type of customer who is more likely to be profitable. This information can be summarized by Portfolio as shown in Table 7.3.

Portfolio Profitability Report

Table 7.3

Sales Portfolio #1	Revenues	Total Cost	Profit $	Profit %
Customer A	$300.00	$162.28	$137.72	46%
Customer B	$360.00	$170.61	$189.39	53%
Total:	$660.00	$332.89	$327.11	50%

Table 7.3 shows that this portfolio of customers has a 50% profit and contributes $327 to the bottom line. But one customer is more profitable than the other. If a Sales Executive wanted to know why, he would simply drill down to see the differences between the two customers. Naturally, this would be the Customer Profitability Report shown in the previous example. To find other profitable Products and services to cross sell, Sales Executives might also look at the Product Profitability Report that will be discussed next.

Tip:

Each customer and customer portfolio are generally assigned to a department. If so, then portfolio profitability of all assigned customers would be the same as the department's profitability. This assignment of customers to departments eliminates the need to create a separate organizational profitability system. You simply summarize customer accounts by department.

Product Profitability

Product Managers are usually responsible for improving the profitability of a Product Line across all customers. They typically look at profitability from the Product and servicing side. Product Managers analyze the processes and seek out improvements to decrease the costs. They would also look for new services to sell and ways to increase revenues or fees. Figure 7.1 shows a high level report for Product Managers.

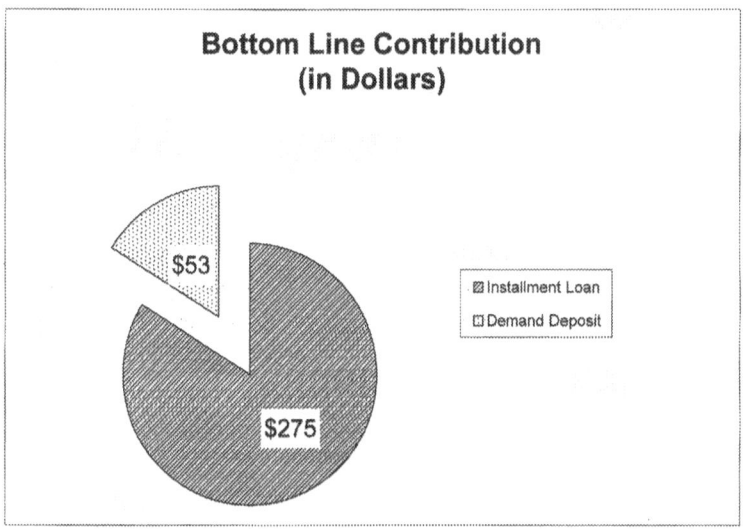

Figure 7.1

Table 7.4

Product	Revenues	Total Cost	Profit $	Profit %
Installment Loan	$600.00	$325.39	$274.61	46%
Demand Deposit	$60.00	$7.50	$52.50	88%

Figure 7.1 and Table 7.4 are summarizations of the transaction profitability by Product. These examples show the Product Manager that the Demand Deposit has an 88% profit whereas the Installment Loans only have a 46%. Two conclusions can be drawn from this. First, the Sales Executives should be cross selling Demand Deposit accounts. Second, the ABM Team should look into improving (decreasing) the costs on Installment Loans. Loans already contribute significant dollars to the bottom line. So, improving the origination and servicing processes for Installment Loans might be an even bigger improvement than cross-selling Demand Deposits. The next step is to drill down by each Product to see which Cost Drivers contribute costs and revenues.

Table 7.5

Installment Loan	Revenues	Total Cost	Profit $	Profit %
Originate a Loan	$500.00	$234.00	$266.00	53%

Table 7.5 (Continued)

Installment Loan	Revenues	Total Cost	Profit $	Profit %
Account Support	$100.00	$90.00	$10.00	10%
Initiate a Payment	$0.00	$1.11	($1.11)	0%
	$600.00	$325.11	$274.89	46%
Demand Deposit	**Revenues**	**Total Cost**	**Profit $**	**Profit %**
Account Support	$60.00	$7.50	$52.50	88%
	$60.00	$7.50	$52.50	88%

The Product Manager might also drill down to the customer level to see which customers use the Products and what their profitability is.

Table 7.6

Installment Loan	Customer	Revenues	Total Service Cost	Profit $	Profit %
Account Support	Customer A	$50	$45	$5	10%
Account Support	Customer A	$50	$45	$5	10%
Account Support	Customer A	$70	$45	$25	36%
		$170	$135	$35	21%

Drilling down one more time the transaction level would bring the Product Manager back to the Transaction Profitability Report shown in Table 7.1. This type of information can also be cross-referenced with customer profiles for a market analysis. Cross-referencing ABM information with customer profiles helps marketing determine the characteristics of profitable customers. Armed with this information, you can better target your marketing and sales.

Finally, Product Managers can dig deeper into the Product's ABC cost by looking at the ABC Cost Breakdown Report. The ABC Cost Breakdown Report helps you analyze the cost and strategize areas for improvement. A sample of the ABC Cost Breakdown Report is reprinted below.

ABC Cost Breakdown Report

Table 7.7

Originate a Loan Process	Department	ABC Cost
Sub-Driver: Complete Application	Branch	$25.75
Sub-Driver: Mail to Loan Operations	Branch	$1.50
Sub-Driver: Process Application	Loan Processing	$2.25
Sub-Driver: Underwriter Approval	Underwriting	$6.75
Sub-Driver: Mail back to Branch	Underwriting	$1.50
Sub-Driver: Book Loan	Branch	$50.75
Sub-Driver: Mail to Loan Operations	Branch	$1.50
Subtotal: Originate a Loan		**$90.00**
Sub-Driver: Idle Capacity (15% x $90.00)	Idle Capacity	$13.50
Sub Driver: SG&A (15% x $90.00)	SG&A	$13.50
Total: Originate a Loan		**$117.00**

Based on the ABC Cost Breakdown Report, the team would focus on:

1. Big Hitters—Complete an Application and Book a Loan

2. Minimize transportation and handoffs—Mail to Loan Operations, Mail back to Branch

3. Sell into idle capacity

4. Participate and encourage improvements in SG&A departments

Another report that can be shared between Sales Executives and Product Managers is the Profit Matrix. The Profit Matrix shows which Customer-Service combinations are profitable. This matrix can be used for analyzing and eliminating un-profitable services. A sample matrix is shown in Table 7.8.

Profit Matrix

Table 7.8

	Customer A	Customer B	Customer C	Customer D	Total
Service 1	$0	-$20,000	$0	$0	-$20,000
Service 2	-$65,000	$20,000	$100,000	-$85,000	-$30,000
Service 3	$250,000	$0	$150,000	$90,000	$490,000
Total	$185,000	$0	$250,000	$5,000	$440,000

It is also helpful to highlight (shade) the High Profile (most valued) Customers on the Profit Matrix. In this case, Customer A and Customer C are highlighted as High Profile Customers for ABI. Product Managers utilize the Profit Matrix to decide which Products to discontinue and which to re-price. In this case, Service 1 can be safely eliminated. It is un-profitable and is not utilized by any of the High Profile Customers. Another option might be to re-price this service. If that's not possible, eliminate it.

Service 2 is used by several High Profile Customers (A & C). Eliminating the service might jeopardize ABI's relationship with these two customers. So, ABI Corporation must consider other options. For example, they can look for ways to improve the costs on Service 2 or increase the amount being charged to Customers A and D (re-price). Alternatively, the Product Manager could try to migrate the customers to more profitable distribution channels for the same service or even out-source it. Any of these options could increase Product and customer profitability. As a last resort, there may be some services where ABI decides to accept a net loss or to give the service away. Running a service at a loss is sometimes done to retain several High Profile Customers. But, this must be a conscious decision and the Profit Matrix is a valuable tool for this analysis.

Departmental Reports

Department and profit center managers need to see the ABC costing information from an operational viewpoint. Recall the ABI example reprinted below from Table 6.7.

Activity Based Management Report

Table 7.9

Expense Category	Fixed/ Variable	Actual Expense	Activity Based Cost	Variance ($)	Variance (%)
Labor	Variable	$124,800	$100,000	$24,800	24.80%
Benefits	Variable	$41,600	$33,000	$8,600	26.06%
Total Personnel:		**$166,400**	**$133,000**	**$33,400**	**25.11%**
Repairs & Support	Variable	$650	$700	($50)	-7.14%
Equipment Depreciation	Fixed	$3,800	$3,700	$100	2.70%
Occupancy	Fixed	$5,800	$5,550	$250	4.50%
Total Property and Equipment:		**$10,250**	**$9,950**	**$300**	**3.02%**
Telecommunications	Variable	$1,100	$900	$200	22.22%
Outside Services	Variable	$100	$75	$25	33.33%
Legal & Professional	Fixed	$200	$150	$50	33.33%
Transportation	Variable	$1,200	$900	$300	33.33%
Printing & Supplies	Variable	$900	$800	$100	12.50%
Total Other Expenses:		**$3,500**	**$2,825**	**$675**	**23.89%**
Total Expenses:		**$180,150**	**$145,775**	**$34,375**	**23.58%**

This report is the most common and traditional look for ABM. Department managers review the Activity Based Management Report on a regular basis to keep tight control over costs and capacity. If their expenses are out of line compared to the ABC costs, it will show up on this report as a large variance. Comparing over several periods, managers may also notice some trends. In either case, the department manager can call the ABM Team to discuss the situation and update the costs, if necessary. Departments are doing a good job at managing costs when they are able to stay within 15% (or whatever limit you set).

Activity Based Management Team Reports

The Activity Based Management Team must have access to each of the reports above. The reports are useful for research and to enable them to see the information from the user's perspective. The Activity Based Management Team also uses several custom reports to stay proactive in maintaining the ABC costs. The first report is the Organizational ABC Variance Report. This report (Table 7.10) compares variances by department and reporting period.

Organizational ABC Variance Report

Table 7.10

	Period 1			Period 2		
	Actual Expenses	Total ABC Cost	Variance	Actual Expenses	Total ABC Cost	Variance
Dept A	$200,000	$180,000	$20,000	$190,000	$170,000	$20,000
Dept B	$180,150	$145,775	$34,375	$146,000	$78,000	$68,000
Dept C	$35,500	$30,000	$5,500	$34,000	$25,000	$9,000
Dept D	$215,000	$205,000	$10,000	$210,000	$205,000	$5,000
Total:	$630,650	$560,775	$69,875	$580,000	$478,000	$102,000

The Organizational ABC Variance Report shows how well the different areas are doing compared to their total ABC costs. This type of report may also be used by middle managers that have several department managers reporting to them. A quick glance shows that the variances increased overall from Period 1 to Period 2. Furthermore, the bulk of the increase is due to Department B. The ABM Team or the manager can then drill down on Department B to the line items. This drill down allows them to see the exact resources causing the variance for a specific department. The detailed report is called the Department ABC Variance Report. It is essentially a variation of the Activity Based Management Report used by department managers. Some groups combine the two reports for simplicity. In this case, the ABM Team notices that the variance is due to labor. This is shown in Table 7.11.

Department ABC Variance Report

Table 7.11

	Period 1		Period 2		Variance ($)	
Expense Category	**Actual Expense**	**Activity Based Cost**	**Actual Expense**	**Activity Based Cost**	**Period 1**	**Period 2**
Labor	$124,800	$100,000	$100,000	$50,000	$24,800	$50,000
Benefits	$41,600	$33,000	$33,000	$16,500	$8,600	$16,500
Total Personnel:	**$166,400**	**$133,000**	**$133,000**	**$66,500**	**$33,400**	**$66,500**
Repairs & Support	$650	$700	$600	$600	($50)	$0
Equipment Depreciation	$3,800	$3,700	$3,000	$2,500	$100	$500
Occupancy	$5,800	$5,550	$5,900	$5,200	$250	$700
Total Property and Equipment:	**$10,250**	**$9,950**	**$9,500**	**$8,300**	**$300**	**$1,200**
Telecommuni-cations	$1,100	$900	$1,100	$1,200	$200	($100)
Outside Ser-vices	$100	$75	$50	$50	$25	$0
Legal & Pro-fessional	$200	$150	$250	$175	$50	$75
Transportation	$1,200	$900	$1,200	$1,000	$300	$200
Printing & Supplies	$900	$800	$900	$775	$100	$125
Total Other Expenses:	**$3,500**	**$2,825**	**$3,500**	**$3,200**	**$675**	**$300**

Table 7.11 (Continued)

Expense Category	Period 1		Period 2		Variance ($)	
	Actual Expense	Activity Based Cost	Actual Expense	Activity Based Cost	Period 1	Period 2
Total Expenses:	$180,150	$145,775	$146,000	$78,000	$34,375	$68,000

The Department ABC Variance Report helps the ABM Team focus its search on the root cause of the variance. Once the cause is found, the Activity Based Management Team can update the ABC costs. In this case, they focus on the production labor. The team might look for changes in processes, activity times, *etc.* Then the team would update the costs accordingly.

The team can do the same type of analysis by drilling down from the Product side. This is done by starting at the Product Manager's report (Bottom Line Contribution) and drilling down to the department level. The result is the same data as displayed above.

The third report specifically designed for the Activity Based Management Team is the ABC Aging report. This report shows all the departments for which ABC costs have been identified and when the data was last updated. It is a proactive approach to prioritizing ABC studies. Sorting the ABC Aging Report by "Last ABC Update" shows which costs are the oldest. An example of the ABC Aging Report is shown in Table 7.12.

ABC Aging Report

Table 7.12

Department	Last ABC Update	Actual Expenses (6 Months)	ABC Costs (6 Months)	Variance
Insurance	Apr-99	$275,000	$255,000	$20,000
Account Reconciliation	Jan-01	$325,000	$240,000	$85,000
Underwriting	Jan-02	$450,250	$410,000	$40,250
Wires	Feb-02	$280,000	$240,000	$40,000
Call Center	May-02	$1,750,000	$1,365,000	$385,000

Table 7.12 (Continued)

Department	Last ABC Update	Actual Expenses (6 Months)	ABC Costs (6 Months)	Variance
Branch	Jun-02	$550,000	$335,500	$214,500
Loan Processing	Oct-02	$260,000	$247,000	$13,000
ATM	Jan-03	$1,550,000	$1,007,500	$542,500
Cash Vault	Sep-03	$750,000	$675,000	$75,000
Lockbox	Nov-03	$750,000	$675,000	$75,000
Web Services	Dec-03	$1,450,000	$841,000	$609,000
Total		**$8,390,250**	**$6,291,000**	**$2,099,250**

The actual expenses and the ABC costs for the last six months are also included to help prioritize the planning of updated studies. An older date and a higher variance is a sign that a new study is needed. In the example above, Account Reconciliation, Call Center, and Branch would need to be updated.

SG&A Reports

Corporations often want a more detailed breakdown of what is included in the SG&A costs. This information is typically shown on an SG&A Breakdown Report. For example, let's say that 15% ($5,750,000) of ABI's expenses were SG&A.

SG&A Breakdown Report

	SG&A Cost	% of Total Expense
Information Technology	$2,600,000	6.78%
Sales	$900,000	2.35%
Accounting	$725,000	1.89%
Human Resources	$600,000	1.57%
Finance	$350,000	0.91%

	SG&A Cost	% of Total Expense
Audit and Legal	$300,000	0.78%
Accounts Payable	$275,000	0.72%
Total	**$5,750,000**	**15.00%**

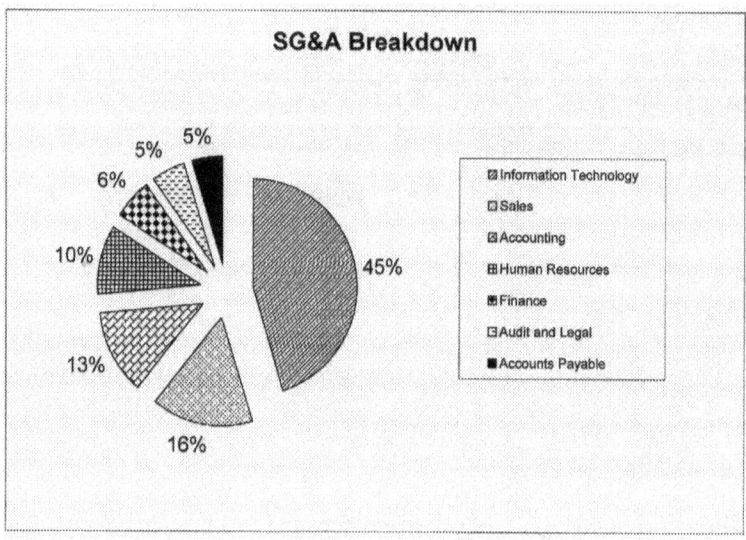

Figure 7.2

The SG&A Breakdown shows the 15% SG&A broken into its component parts. It shows how much is contributed by each overhead area and can be linked to other reports as desired. The SG&A Breakdown also shows a pie graph with the percent of the total SG&A that each slice represents. Again, this is a very simple report. However, this type of analysis provides a wealth of information and inspiration to decision makers.

Step Eight: Take Action!

AKA: "Killing Your Costs"—How to use ABM to Lead your Company into a Competition Crushing Machine.

Okay, we have talked about setting up the system, performing studies, rolling up the costs, and many of the roadblocks to avoid. Now comes the fun part. Some people call this process improvement. We call it "Killing Your Costs".

Using ABC and the Resource Costing Method explained in this book, you have all the tools and information you need to manage a business. The first part is knowing what it should cost using the current processes and practices (ABC). The second part is using the information to manage and improve your organization (ABM). Lastly, update your costs and begin again. Don't forget this last step. You must keep your costs in sync with your process improvements; otherwise, the reports will be meaningless. So managing through ABM is only half the battle. The other half is driving ahead and improving your processes.

Many people try to improve by cutting costs. They hope that it will improve their ratios and make the stock look good to investors. This a very short term approach. Costs are like weeds. Once they take hold, they are a devil to get rid of. Merely cutting them won't solve anything. They'll grow back. What you really want is to kill them! Kill them at the roots! Kill them so they won't come back. Kill your costs. That is the essence of process improvement and that is when you move from Managing to Leading.

The answers are out there. All you just have to do is put on your thinking cap. Go to the Gemba (where the work is performed) and look at things from a process improvement perspective. Often consultants and outsiders can help you see the forest through the trees. But in the end, it is the leaders of your company that must make the changes and launch the revolutions from within. No one else can do that for you.

One of the best moves you can make is to use your Activity Based Management team for both maintaining <u>and</u> improving costs. There are two key reasons for this. First, as the ABM Team develops the original ABC costs, they often notice activities and opportunities for immediate improvement. Done correctly, on-the-spot improvements create a lot of goodwill. This goodwill can make future projects in the area go a lot smoother.

Second, using the Activity Based Management Team to calculate costs and improve processes is more efficient than two separate groups. It is more efficient because they already know the people and the processes from the original ABC Study. As the cost studies are performed, the team learns a lot about the responsibilities and functions of the area. This familiarity allows them to more quickly analyze and improve the processes. It also gives them an excellent background when working with other areas that are upstream or downstream of the original department. The team can look for common trends, handoffs, duplications of effort or actions in one area that may cause problems or rework in another.

Having said that, remember that familiarity with the process does not make them experts in the process. The ABM Team will be familiar with the process, which is good. But, the real experts are the people who do the work every day. The team will always need the experts' input/ideas on changes and improvements. Some of the best ideas will come from the process experts. So, gathering and utilizing the input will create buy-in and ownership in the new process. It will also increase the chances that the improvements will be successfully implemented.

Tip:

Word of mouth (and a little publicity in the company newsletter) will create demand for improvement in other areas. Many areas desire improvement, but lack the time, resources or expertise. Therefore, good publicity and a positive track record will create an upward spiral of demand for the team. The increasing demand for the team's services will pave the way for adding more resources and creating an even bigger impact on the bottom line.

In the remainder of this section, we'll cover several topics to help improve your organization. These topics are summarized below.

1. Activity Based Budgeting and Planning (ABB/P)

2. Break-Even Analysis

3. Labor Capacity Management

4. Occupancy Capacity Management

5. Staff Estimates

6. Using Summary and Credit Departments

7. Finding More Help—Using Consultants

8. Process Improvement Techniques—improving SG&A areas, Benchmarking, Bottleneck Analysis (TOC), Six Sigma, and Value Added Analyses

ACTIVITY BASED BUDGETING AND PLANNING (ABB/P)

Once under way with Activity Based Management, another use of your ABC information is in Budgeting and Planning. Managers normally plan their budgets using their expense or General Ledger lines. ABB/P is a little different. In ABB/P, you plan the volumes for the Cost Drivers. The planned volumes can then be multiplied by the ABC cost to estimate the budgeted expenses. The reason is that the planned Cost Driver volumes represent the expected level of demand for the corporation's services. These services require resources (labor, equipment time, *etc.*) and the resources must be paid for (expense). Thus, the planned demand volume causes the planned expense.

The beauty of it, is that the calculation has already be been built in your ABM system. You already multiply your volumes * ABC cost for each resource on a regular basis. You are simply changing the source of the volumes from actual (real) volumes to planned volumes. Include a planned idle capacity percentage and you have an excellent start on a budget. A budget that the operational managers know they can live by, because they already do in ABM.

There are several tips to help focus this process. The key word being: "*Focus*". You want to make the process as smooth and painless as possible for managers. Planning every little detail is a waste of time. ABB/P budgeting may be more reflective of the resources required, but it is still based on an assumed demand for your services. It is an estimate. If the volume or mix of services demanded differs from the budget (as it inevitably does) then the budget will naturally have a variance compared to the actual expenses. So, don't go over board on the time spent for budgeting. Fortunately, focus can be easily attained in your ABB/P system through a little creativity and foresight. Below are some simple examples of how to do this.

1. Assume starting volumes—Provide the users with tentative/assumed volumes. This tentative volume can be last year's total volume (assuming no increases) or last year's volume plus 5% increase across the board, *etc*. This one step will save the greatest amount of time in planning. If all else fails, the default volume will be used.

2. Focus on the big hitters—Typically, a small number of Cost Drivers make up the top 60-80% of the costs. Focus on these items first.

3. Focus on the largest volumes. The largest volumes may not have the highest total cost. However, any large fluctuations in high volume services could cause a major impact on the overall cost and operational efficiencies. So, focus the largest volumes second.

4. Adjust volumes for any major changes (Product launches, *etc*.) that are planned for the next year. Plan these third.

5. Leave the rest as the default (assumed) volumes.

The steps listed above will save the users input time and focus their efforts on the most important items. This focus can be critical during the budget season when resources are already stretched thin. You simply assume the starting volumes, then have users adjust the big hitters, plan the highest volume items, and adjust for any big changes they expect in the coming year. The rest of the volumes can be left as the assumed values. Chances are good that any changes in the remaining services will have little impact on the bottom line or operations.

Occasionally, new Product launches will require the adding of new Cost Drivers and estimated costs into the ABC and ABB/P system. That's fine. Product Managers often make this request as they prepare pro-forma profitability for the coming year. The pro-forma profitability for any new Products will require an estimated cost per item. Since the Activity Based Management Team will have to do this for the pro-forma anyway, you might as well add it to the ABB/P system.

The calculation:

The ABB/P calculation is the same method used to calculate the ABC costs. The only difference is that you multiply the resource ABC cost (from ABC) by the projected volume not the actual volume. Then you add in the idle capacity and SG&A to get the budgeted expenses by GL Line. Again, this can all be done automatically by the ABM system. In the end, managers have a clear of idea of the costs and amount of resources that will be required for the next year. The best part is that ABB/P is actionable information. Managers can compare their current resources to ABB to look for any large differences. Then they make a plan to hire, promote, purchase, or attrition resources as appropriate.

Tip:

An alternative technique is to use ABB/P as a budget validation tool. First, plan the expenses using the traditional budgeting methods. Then, the Sales and Product Management Teams plan the volumes. Finally, run ABB/P and compare the ABB/P results with the expenses planned using the traditional budgeting methodology. This approach is a great way to validate the budget. It also ensures the right amount of resources are included in the plan to account for the expected changes.

ABB/P for Rolling Forecasts

A Rolling Forecast is when a company continuously plans their financials for a rolling 12 or 18 months. Of course, this is very easy to do with ABB/P. It is the same methodology shown above except you'll run the calculation every month or every quarter instead of annually.

Who should plan the volumes?

Typically, Product Managers, Sales Executives, or Business Units leaders plan the volumes. Operational managers are often aware of how sales are going and what will be implemented in the next year. But the Product Managers have better visibility to the marketing and sales side, so their estimates should be closer to the actual. The Product Manager and Sales Executive's estimates are also used for planning profit margins and, in the long run, they are held accountable for these numbers. In this sense, ABB/P provides a good check and balance similar to ABM.

Another reason the operations folks should not plan volumes is that a particular Product or service often touches multiple departments. If each department planned its own volume, then, inevitably, the departments that work on the same service will not have matching volumes. Reconciling these differences requires additional effort, time, and resources to come to agreement on the volumes.

Finally, ABB/P increases the communication between operations, Sales and Product Management. As mentioned above, it sticks out like a sore thumb when the ABB/P costs don't match the planned expenses or when the planned resources are significantly different than the current amount of resources. Through ABB/P this can be immediately seen and resolved through open dialogue between the appropriate parties.

Planning for SG&A and Overhead Departments

SG&A and overhead departments should budget the traditional way. An alternative method is to budget by taking a quick survey of the internal users of their SG&A services to see how much demand there will be in the next year. Then you can plan the SG&A's budget based on the estimated service demand. This technique is similar to planning ABB/P based on volumes. Most corporations then hold the overhead departments accountable for meeting/beating their budgets. More information on improving SG&A departments can be found in the Process Improvement portion of Taking Action.

Monitoring Performance Compared to Budget

Monitoring performance compared to the ABB/P is easy with ABM. You can do this by setting up reports similar to the customer, Product and departmental reports (see Reporting section in Step Seven). The only difference is that you'll be comparing actual expenses to ABB/P instead of ABC costs. Alternatively, you could set up the reports to compare all three side by side (actual expense, ABB, and ABC costs).

BREAK-EVEN ANALYSIS

Product Managers, and others involved in pricing, are often concerned with what volume needs to be sold to cover all the costs (fixed and variable). This is referred to as the break-even quantity. It is a very straightforward calculation. First, remember that the profit is calculated as:

Profit = (SP * Vol) - (VC * Vol) - FC

Where:

SP = Selling Price
Vol = Volume

VC = Variable ABC Cost
FC = Total Fixed Costs

Solving for the volume:

Profit + FC = (SP * Vol) - (VC * Vol)
Profit + FC = (SP - VC) * Vol
(Profit + FC)/(SP - VC) = Vol

Or

Vol = (Profit + FC)/(SP - VC)

The break-even volume is minimum volume at which the selling price covers all the variable and fixed costs. Therefore, at the break-even point, the profit would be zero.

Vol = (0 + FC)/(SP - VC)

Vol = FC/(SP - VC)

Simply plug in the total fixed costs, selling price, and variable ABC cost from ABM, and you'll have the break-even volume.

People generally make two modifications to this. First, the selling price is usually the average selling price or some other representative (weighted average) price. This is often done when the Price is negotiated differently for each large customer. The second modification is on the profit. In real life, Sales teams are not rewarded for breaking even (0 profitability). Instead, their targets are to hit a certain level (or %) of profitability. With this in mind, you can modify the break-even calculation to account for the desired profitability (PM * SP).

Vol = FC/(SP - VC - (PM * SP))

Where PM = Profit Margin (i.e. desired profitability %)

Lets look at a quick example from ABI. Lets say the Product Manager for Service X wants to know how many customer transactions he'll need, to achieve a 15% profit on a given service. He knows that the average selling price for a particular service is $10 per transaction, the variable ABC cost is $6 per transaction, and the total fixed cost is $100,000. The manager plugs these numbers into the calculation as follows:

Vol = ($100,000)/($10 - $6 - ($10 * 15%))

Vol = 40,000 Transactions

So, the Product Manager needs to sell at least 40,000 transactions with an average selling price of at least $10 each to ensure a 15% profit.

Tip:

Not sure what the total fixed cost is? Multiply the fixed ABC cost by the volume for the last 12 months to get the total fixed cost. Since this is a volume-based cost, most people also factor in the idle capacity (15%) into the total fixed cost.

Tip:

Ensure that the volumes and costs cover the same length of time. For example, if you are using annualized volumes, then you should use the annualized fixed cost. Otherwise, you will get incorrect results.

LABOR CAPACITY MANAGEMENT

Idle labor capacity is also called unused capacity and excess capacity depending on your viewpoint. It is often something managers seek to stamp out. Before you do…read this section!

Idle capacity and capacity management are often misunderstood. Managers and leaders must avoid knee-jerk reactions when viewing the idle capacity reports. Sometimes people are too quick to pull the trigger and cut resources. This is a horrible way to lead. A one-time blip in idle capacity is not a trend and does not justify adverse actions. Rather it indicates a need for closer investigation. Again, this is not an exact science, but then LEADERSHIP never is. Below are a few tips and suggestions.

Calculating Idle Capacity

Idle capacity is the difference between the amount of resources available and the amount needed to complete the services demanded. This is most often done with labor, equipment, occupancy, and storage (electronic system space). Lets look at another ABI example.

Expense Category	Fixed/ Variable	Actual Expense	Activity Based Cost	Variance ($)	Variance (%)
Labor	Variable	$72,800	$60,000	$12,800	21.33%
Benefits	Variable	$14,500	$12,000	$2,500	20.83%
Total Personnel:		**$87,300**	**$72,000**	**$15,300**	**21.25%**

This table shows that the actual labor expenses for Department B at ABI was $72,800 but the Activity Based Cost was only $60,000. That is a 21% difference or idle capacity. This translates to 436 idle hours per year (2,080 hours x 21%) or 7 hours per week.

The manager has been noticing the same item for the past couple of reporting periods. He has already reviewed the activity times and feels comfortable that this variance is representative of the current work levels in his department. So, he decides that he'll loan out one of his employees for up to one day per week until the situation changes. Once this is done <u>and</u> the employee's salary for that time is charged to the other department the results might resemble Table 8.1.

Table 8.1

Expense Category	Fixed/ Variable	Actual Expense	Activity Based Cost	Variance ($)	Variance (%)
Labor	Variable	$65,440	$60,500	$4,940	8.17%
Benefits	Variable	$13,500	$12,100	$1,400	11.57%
Total Personnel:		**$78,940**	**$72,600**	**$6,340**	**8.73%**

As it turns out the manager was only able to loan the employee out for partial day each week. However, notice how loaning the employee out for just a part of a day changes the entire picture. Charging the time to the other department reduces labor by $7,360 to $65,440. Benefits are based on the salaries and head-count so they reduce automatically as well. Note: you usually don't have to do this yourself because it is set-up to calculate through the HR and accounting systems automatically. In this case, the overall Personnel Variance decreased to 8.73%.

It is important for the Activity Based Management Team to learn the method for managers to loan folks out. You need to know how managers can do this, whom to talk to in HR and how to correctly charge the time. Managers will be leery to do this unless there is a process in place and there are very clear instructions on how to do it. So, the Activity Based Management Team must develop an easy way for managers to do this with minimal effort.

How much idle capacity is acceptable?

The amount of acceptable idle capacity varies. Different industries, companies, and even departments require different levels. Most groups find that 10-15% idle capacity provides enough room for vacations, sick days, and volume fluctuations. The Human Resources department can give you an idea of your company's average for vacations, personal, and sick days. HR might also be able to provide industry averages. Areas with greater proportions of fixed costs (i.e. Information Technology, automated/machine intensive departments *etc.*) may also need a higher level of acceptable idle capacity. Remember the ABM method presented in this book is self-managing, just follow the steps, and watch the leaders excel.

Managing the idle capacity

First, look for trends. Ask yourself: Is the idle capacity decreasing, increasing, or remaining level? How long has this trend been happening? and Is it a seasonal fluctuation or industry driven? Three or four consistent months are usually enough for trending. Although, longer periods may be necessary, if seasonality comes into play.

Good leaders will see trends forming, take incremental actions, and avoid sudden knee jerk decisions. For example, if the idle capacity is increasing, or remains level but needs to be reduced, a good leader may start loaning people out (and charging the time out) to other departments that need the help. This would give the employee meaningful, valuable work, reduce the department's idle capacity, and help the other department avoid the expense of interviewing, hiring, and training a new employee.

Here are some other suggestions to consider:

Symptom (Trend)	**Suggestions**
Increasing idle capacity	• Loan employees out to other departments—this will increase their skills, and give them valuable, meaningful work to perform. It will also save other departments the expense of interviewing, hiring, and training a new employee. Just remember to charge their loaned time to the other department.
	• Share technology or other fixed resources with several areas and share the cost based on consumption (ABM-Resource Costing).
	• Reduction through attrition. As employees leave, retire or get promoted, don't replace them. Typically, attrition runs 5-10% per year. See your Human Resources department for the most up to date turnover rates in your company or industry.
	• Utilize the extra time for Training, Process, and Productivity Improvements. This is especially valuable when the idle capacity is temporary. For example, you can use the time to improve the area and prepare for the next big push. Use the time to rehearse and improve machine set-up times or train employees how to spot common errors and troubleshoot solutions, *etc*. Use the time to brainstorm and implement productivity and quality improvements.
	• Advertise excess availability to the Sales Team. This is especially true when idle capacity appears to be a long-term trend. Let them know you can take on more business. Note: make sure you can deliver on this promise. There is nothing worse than spending a lot of time winning a large client only to find out you can't provide good consistent service. Also, check departments up and downstream to ensure they can handle the extra workload as well. Hitting your local optimum doesn't always optimize the overall process.

Symptom (Trend)	*Suggestions*
Constant idle capacity	• See suggestions for increasing idle capacity. They hold true here as well.
Decreasing idle capacity	• You Need Process and Productivity Improvement!
	• Check to see if this is an industry trend or just an upturn in your company.
	• Borrow employees from other departments. They already know the company, how to get to work, already receive the benefits, and probably know some of the bigger customers. All you'll have to do is train them. Also, make sure you take care of them. Use the loaned employees for valuable, meaningful work. Give them the same praise and recognition as your other employees. Remember loaned employees long for job enrichment and increasing job skills like everyone else. Keep that in mind as training opportunities arise.
	• Hire "Temporary to Permanent" or "Temp to Hire" employees through an employment agency or contract services firm. The nice part is that if you aren't getting good performance out of a temporary, you can get a replacement with one call to the employment agency. Often they can send a replacement the next day. Just make sure you tell the employment firm why you want a replacement. Constructive feedback will help them to better fulfill your needs in the future.

The great part about Resource Costing, as presented in this book, is that you can see your idle capacity. You know which departments have idle capacity and what type it is (idle labor, idle machine time, unused occupancy, *etc.*). Below are a few sample reports from ABI, to give you an idea of how you can view this information. These simple graphs can be generated from any ABM system. They can also be produced in spreadsheets or other standalone analysis programs. Figure 8.1 depicts how much idle capacity is costing ABI for a given time period.

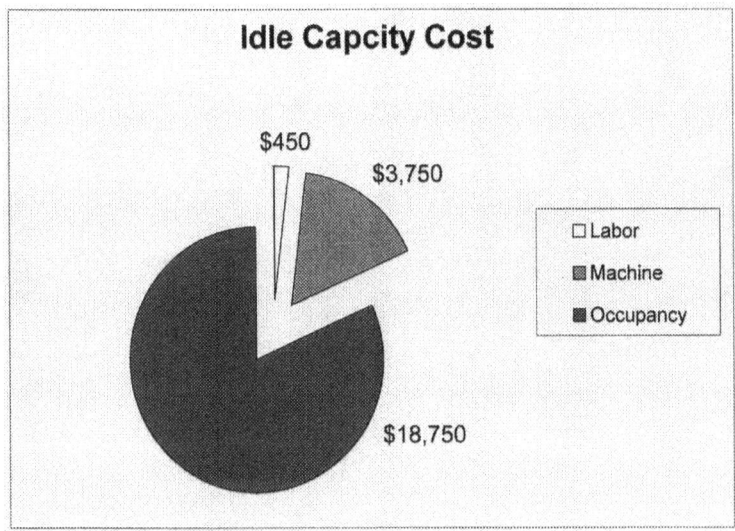

Figure 8.1

The idle capacity cost graph breaks the idle capacity into three categories: labor, machine, and occupancy. As with any of these graphs you may find it more useful to sub-divide some of these categories or to show them by Business Unit, Product or process. They can also be shown as percentages. The next graph (Figure 8.2) shows the idle capacity in relation to the capacity utilization and total capacity.

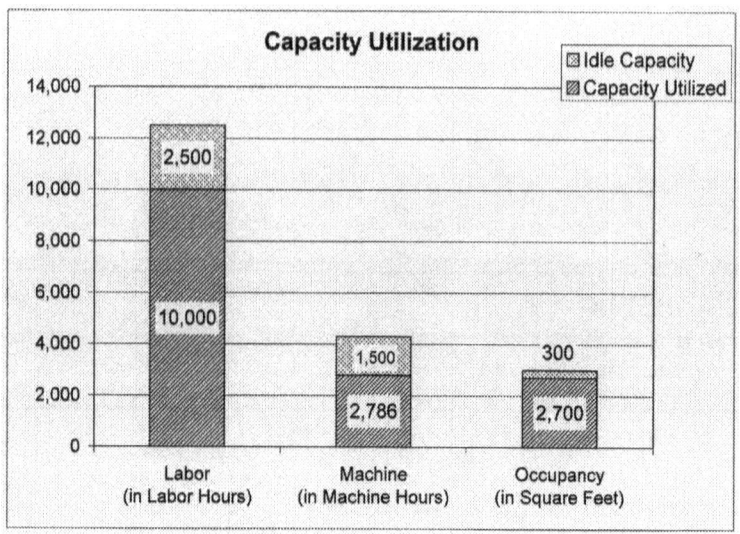

Figure 8.2

Figure 8.2 helps you understand how the idle capacity relates to the overall capacity of the department, or Business Unit. The total capacity is the sum of the idle and utilized capacity. The next graph (below) is an example of trending. Again, don't make knee jerk decisions based on one reporting period. Watch for trends like that shown in Figure 8.3.

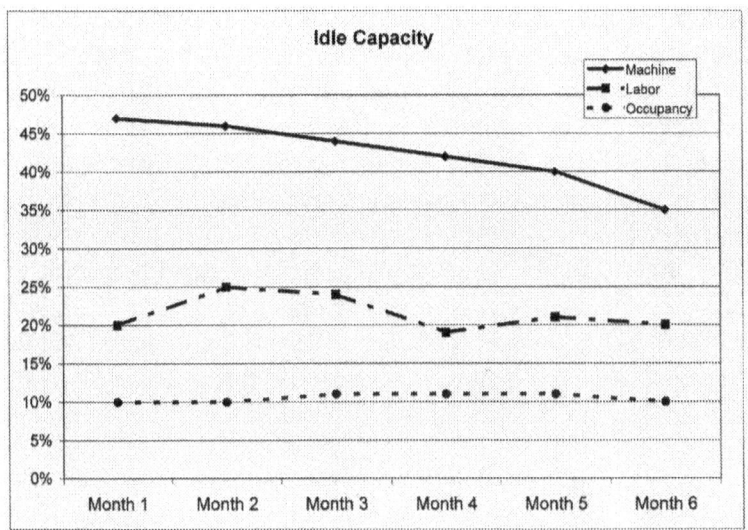

Figure 8.3

Notice the southeasterly (downward) trend on the machine idle capacity. This is a definite indicator. Leaders must be proactive and do a quick analysis to see what is causing this trend. You can look at both industry and market trends. Decide see if this will continue and if the machines will become more loaded as time goes on. If so, take action quickly! It can take a great deal of time to research, select, request, get approval, purchase, install, test, and implement a new system or processing machine. In the mean time, workarounds and Productivity Improvements should be researched in case the new machines don't arrive in time. You may find out the improvements alone will offset the trend. This can save you money and make your company more competitive.

Increasing your capacity

Capacity increase projects are a double-edged sword. If you are truly over capacity and there are more transactions or customers than you have hours in the day, then take on a process improvement project with the goal of increasing you capacity. However, if this is not the case then you may have other priorities that you need to be working on. For example, recall that profitability is calculated as:

Profit   = Revenue - Total Cost
             = Revenue - (Total ABC Cost + Idle Capacity + SG&A)

Now, let's say you undertake a project to increase your capacity by decreasing your ABC activity time (processing time per item). This decrease in resources (time) required per item will decrease the ABC cost. It will also free up a lot more processing labor. This unoccupied labor time is actually idle labor and, thus, the idle capacity cost will increase. The net result is that the total cost to the company is the same as it was before the improvement. You only moved the cost from one bucket to another (from total ABC cost to idle capacity).

Let's put some numbers behind this. The Activity Based Management Team at ABI was asked to analyze an area and increase the capacity. They know that there are currently 1,000 hours available for this process to operate and that each item takes approximately 1 hour to complete. They look at the ABC information, do some interviews, and follow some of the process improvement techniques presented later in this book. The manager implemented the recommendations and was able to decrease the activity time to 0.45 hours per item, thus increasing the capacity by 122%. Then the team looked up the actual volumes and summarized the information with Figure 8.4.

	Before	After
Activity Time (Hours)	1	0.45
Items Processed	700	700
Hours Required	**700**	**315**

	Before	After
Capacity Utilized (Hours)	700	315
Idle Capacity (Hours)	300	685
Total Capacity (Hours)	**1,000**	**1,000**

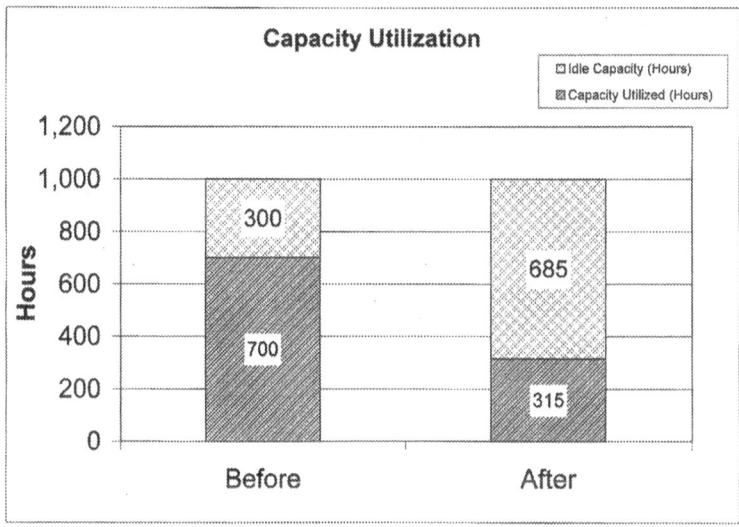

Figure 8.4

The department was only averaging 700 items per month and had 300 hours of idle capacity. The area was nowhere close to their capacity. Increasing their capacity in this case simply moved the hours from one bucket (used capacity) to another (idle capacity). If there is no dramatic increase in volume then the only way to decrease the costs is to loan people out or lay people off. This is one reason why employees cringe at the mention of process improvement. Employees fear it means layoffs and fewer jobs available.

The flip side is that the Activity Based Management Team is also a limited resource. Working on this project means they were not working on something else. In essence, it comes down to prioritization. Focus on projects that have the greatest potential to improve the organization as a whole.

Another way that people try to increase capacity is by purchasing more resources. This works from the sense that more equipment and more labor will enable you to process more items. However, in many situations the increase in revenues you gain from this higher capacity is offset by the increase in costs of the additional labor and equipment. In the end, you may have more revenues, but your overall profitability will be relatively unchanged.

Now, assume that there is pent up demand for the services and you genuinely need more capacity. Again, you undertake a project to increase you capacity by decreasing your activity times, which frees up some of your labor resources. This extra labor will then be used to process more items. In this scenario, the total cost will remain roughly the same (doing more volume with the same resources). However, the increased volume will increase the revenues. Greater revenue for the same cost means your profitability increases.

Tip:

Some people try to charge the cost of purchasing new equipment or labor for increasing their capacity to an administrative department. This approach ends up with the same results as increasing your idle capacity. The difference is that it increases the corporation's SG&A cost. It may be a case of people playing with their numbers to make themselves look good, instead of doing the right thing. If you see this happening let upper management know or make a visit to your internal auditors. It could be a case of fraud when it is used to artificially increase one's bonus payments.

Obviously, we are not saying, "don't make capacity improvements". Just the opposite. It is a good thing to do and should be done on some occasions. Capacity should be increased for only one of two reasons: 1) to decrease the overall costs or 2) to increase revenues by increasing the actual throughput. So, before you undertake a capacity improvement project, consider these questions.

1.   What will you do with the extra capacity?

2.   Will it really be utilized?

3.   If not fully utilized, what will you do with the extra resources?

This is what we call Strategic Leadership. Think ahead about where these resources could be better utilized and start laying the groundwork prior to the implementation of such improvements. The prep work will give the organization a greater sense of security and help the transition go much smoother. Simply saying "Don't worry, we'll find something for you" isn't enough. People need specifics. They need something to look forward to, not to be concerned about being laid off.

OCCUPANCY CAPACITY MANAGEMENT

Occupancy is one of the biggest costs in a company, but few people know how to manage and improve it. Some companies are fortunate enough to have professional facilities managers. If you do not, here are some quick ideas on how to improve your occupancy capacity/costs:

1. Sublease extra space to other companies, thus offsetting some of the costs

2. Move to a cheaper (smaller) location i.e. lower real estate taxes, tax incentives, lower rent, lower insurance rates (based on crime, weather, *etc.*)

3. Consolidate work groups in one location and sell the vacated facilities

4. Switch from many people on one shift, to people split across three shifts sharing the same workspaces. This avoids adding more occupancy space for an increase in staff during market or business upswings.

5. Minimize utility usage (heat or electricity) during off hours

6. Renegotiate the rent, utilities, or tax incentives.

The problem with utilizing each of the items above is how do you measure your used and idle capacity. There are two possible scenarios in occupancy for a given department.

1. A department occupies its own facility and is charged for the total cost of that facility

2. A department shares a facility and is allocated a portion of the total occupancy cost of the facility

In either case, it is based on the number of square feet occupied by the given department. The occupancy costs often include utilities, rent, depreciation, real estate taxes, insurance, maintenance, housekeeping, *etc.* Each of the costing items may be a separate expense line on the General Ledger. In reality, they are very closely related and can be lumped together as "occupancy" when thinking in terms of process improvement.

In the first scenario, a department occupies its own facility or building and is charged for the total expenses of that facility. An example of this might be a branch office for a bank. Each branch has a store unto itself and is charged the total cost of that store. To improve the occupancy cost you could move to a cheaper location, minimize utility usage during off hours, renegotiate contracts, or renegotiate the rent. If you have unused space, you could share it with another group of people from the bank (such as Lenders, or Sales Executives) who might have a need for a local, professional place to meet with clients. If you have idle meeting rooms you could rent them out to community organizations, or host business group luncheons. You might also be able to loan out the space for meetings held by non-profit groups and write it off on your taxes.

In the second scenario, the department shares a building with other departments from the same bank and is apportioned some part of the total occupancy cost. This is often done based on square footage. In this case, you'd want to minimize the footprint or square footage the department occupies, and then update the corporate occupancy and ABC calculations. The less area (square feet) a department occupies, the less occupancy it will be charged.

Measuring Square Feet

A department's footprint is measured in square feet. This is calculated as the length of the area multiplied by the width. Be sure to include all the areas that belong to the department (aisles, storage spaces, personal space, *etc.*). Of course, several tools can help you do this. For example, you can pace off the distance, use a tape measure, or use a rolling pacer. You may also consider a laser range finder like those used by golfers or hunters.

If you do these measurements often, it may be worth your while to invest in a GPS unit. Then you can walk to each corner get the bearing and have it automatically log the data into a spreadsheet. Many of these devices are accurate to less than 1 meter (three feet). One caveat, though, make sure you test one in your facility prior to buying it. Sometimes the GPS units have trouble finding satellites when they are surrounded by concrete and steel.

Finding Idle Occupancy

First and foremost, you need to have a facility layout. The facility layout (or map) is where you label each of the departments, their relative size, and their function. This basic map can be given to any Activity Based Management or Industrial Engineering Team for improvement analysis. These folks often specialize in Facility Layout and Design. For the rest of us, there are several basic options. You can redesign your layout by function, process, work-cells, or work-teams. Many books describe how to properly design facility layouts to achieve maximum efficiency and utilization. So, we will only cover it briefly here.

1.   Functional Layouts try to keep large functional groups together. Keeping functional groups close together makes it easier to manage resources.

2. Process and Work-cell layouts put related workgroups (processes) together. This type of layout increases communication and minimizes handoffs. It also promotes ownership in the service from start to finish.

3. Work-team layouts are often used for standalone areas or areas shared by many groups. The mailroom in a large office complex would be an example of a Work-team.

Tip:

See if the work areas are occupied 24 hours per day or just the standard eight. If the space is occupied for just eight hours per day, then 66% (or 16 hours) is idle each day. Try to share work areas across shifts, to maximize workspace utilization.

The idle capacity is out there; you just have to know where to look. Conserve space wherever applicable, but don't cram things so close together that it is a safety hazard and people are tripping over stuff. Try to minimize the footprints of each department without creating unbearable working conditions. Good facility design books can give you plenty of ideas for establishing standard aisle widths, personal space, *etc.*

STAFF ESTIMATES

Staff Estimates are simple calculations used to estimate the amount of labor resources required for different levels of demand. They are not difficult calculations and won't take a lot of time. Staff Estimates are different from Staffing Models. Staffing Models are much more complicated and statistically oriented. We won't discuss Staffing Models in this book since the statistics, queuing theories, and experimental designs could fill a book by themselves.

Staff Estimates are calculated from the information gained in ABC time studies. You can use Staff Estimates to quickly project staffing requirements after process improvements or adding new services. They are also used for quick ad-hoc analysis and "What-if" scenario comparisons. A sample calculation is shown in Table 8.2.

Table 8.2

	Labor Hours per Transaction	Projected Volume	Total Hours Required	Hours per FTE	FTE Required
Service A	0.0500	2,000	100	2,080	0.05
Service B	0.0026	20,000,000	52,000	2,080	25.00
Service C	0.0030	35,000	105	2,080	0.05
Totals:			52,205		25.10

As you can tell from the Table 8.2, it's a simple calculation. The labor hours for each transaction (activity time) are multiplied by projected annual volume (number of transactions). The result is the total hours required. Then, divide the total hours required by the total annual hours per full time employee (FTE) to get the average number of full time employees required for the coming year. The sum of the FTE for each of the services provided by a department is the total number of people that will be required for the projected volume.

Table 8.2 shows that the true driver of the headcount for this department is Service B. The net requirement, assuming the projected volume and mix of services, is 26 full time employees (always round up). You may also consider adding a factor for idle capacity, vacations, holidays, *etc.* to have a more realistic estimate.

Staff Estimates can be used every week to plan the work schedules. However, this only works when the labor is truly variable and fluctuates with the volume (see Step 6 for more detail on fixed and variable labor). Some organizations use Staff Estimates at a higher level to show how many people are needed across the whole organization. Executives can then plan-ahead to redeploy resources or increase/decrease staffing, as needed.

A variation of Staff Estimates can also be used in conjunction with Activity Based Budgeting/Planning for support areas such as Information Technology, Human Resources or Project Management. For these areas, budgets are typically based on the projects and support that will be required for the upcoming year. These requirements can be put in the Staff Estimate and balanced back to the Budget for validation. This enables planners to see if there is enough resources budgeted for the projected demand of the services.

Once the basic concept of Staff Estimates has been accepted, you can further tailor it to suit your needs. You can add in Key Performance Indicators (KPI), metrics, market factors, and other items to refine the estimate. Just be careful not to make it too complicated.

Tip:

Keep the calculations simple. Complex and cumbersome calculations will not be understood or used correctly (if at all). The goal is to give managers a quick and simple tool to quantify their staffing decisions. Time wasted on over-complicated analyses, can be better spent on process improvement.

Alternative Methods for Staff Estimates

Sometimes an estimate based on activity time isn't appropriate for a particular area. For example, assume you want to create a Staff Estimate for a Sales department. In Sales and other overhead areas, you don't have activity times per sale, activity times per GL Account balanced, *etc.* Instead, other productivity metrics can be used to estimate your staffing levels. A few of these are listed below:

1. Revenues per FTE

2. Number of Customer Accounts per FTE

3. Average Assets ($) per FTE

4. Number of Employees Supported per FTE

Many SG&A areas will use ratios similar to the ones above to create a Staff Estimate. These ratios usually represent annualized numbers or averages. For example, lets say ABI uses revenues per FTE as a productivity measure for their Sales folks. Assuming the Sales Group has $15,000,000 in annual revenue and 20 full time Sales folks the following calculation can be performed.

Table 8.3

	Current Revenue	Current FTE	Avg Revenue per FTE
Current Level	$15,000,000	20	$750,000

The average revenue per FTE is calculated as the current revenue divided by the current FTE. The average revenue per FTE can then be used to estimate the number of Sales folks needed to reach the revenue growth targets. Such a target might be an increase (growth) in Sales of 10%, 15% or 20%. Several sales growth scenarios can be calculated for comparison as shown in Table 8.4.

Table 8.4

Revenue Growth Target (%)	Revenue Growth Target ($)	Avg Revenue per FTE	FTE Required
Increase 10%	$16,500,000	$750,000	22
Increase 15%	$17,250,000	$750,000	23
Increase 20%	$18,000,000	$750,000	24

The revenue growth target (in dollars) is the current revenue from Table 8.3, multiplied by the desired increase (10%, 15% or 20%). The average revenue per FTE is derived from the current level of revenues and FTE as calculated in Table 8.3. Finally, the FTE Required is the revenue growth target (in dollars) divided by the average revenue per FTE and rounding up to the next whole employee.

Notice that this calculation assumes there has been no process improvements in the Sales area and that there have been no other changes. It can be used as an ad-hoc estimate or rule of thumb. This calculation can also be performed with any productivity measure or a combination of measures. Just don't make it too complicated or difficult to understand.

USING SUMMARY OR CREDIT DEPARTMENTS

"Summary Departments" or credit areas are sometimes created for reporting purposes. These departments are created with the intention of being able to see the credit for all the work performed by a given Business Unit in one "Summary Department". Another variation is to combine the costs of several departments during the ABC Study and assign the combined ABC cost to only one of them. This is done with the best intentions. Unfortunately, these are flawed designs and don't work for ABM.

"Summary Departments" cause you to lose all the drill down and traceability required for successful Activity Based Management. Traceability is key to understanding what makes up the cost and for holding people accountable. If you can't trace a variance back to its source then the report is not actionable and you cannot manage by it. To illustrate this point, consider an example from ABI.

Early in their ABC Studies, the Activity Based Management Team found four inter-related departments (A, B, C, and D). Due to their close proximity and the fact that they are dependent on one another, the Team mistakenly decides to combine all the costs into a "Summary Department". After several reporting periods with ABM (Volume * ABC Cost), the results resemble those in Table 8.5.

Table 8.5

	Period 1			Period 2		
	Actual Expenses	*Total ABC Cost*	*Variance*	*Actual Expenses*	*Total ABC Cost*	*Variance*
Dept A	$200,000			$190,000		
Dept B	$180,150			$146,000		
Dept C	$35,500			$34,000		
Dept D	$215,000			$210,000		
Summary Dept:	$630,650	$560,775	$69,875	$580,000	$478,000	$102,000

Notice that the "Summary Department" is an aggregate of departments A, B, C, and D. When the team wants to know how well the costs are being managed (Activity Based Management) they learn very little. In period 1, they know that there is $69,875 ($630,650 - $560,775) in variance. Is this idle capacity? If so, what kind (labor, machine, or occupancy)? Where is the idle capacity? Is it across the board (equal amounts in A, B, and C) or is the bulk of it in one department?

If you do Resource Costing on this summary department, you may know whether it is labor or equipment that is causing the problem, but you still won't know where it is (Department A, B, or C). Not knowing the origin creates a headache for the Activity Based Management Team and adds no value to system. Also, since no one knows where the variance came from, no one can be held responsible for improving it. The ABC costs must be reflective of the department that consumes the resources. If not, then the report is useless. You'll know, in aggregate, what the variance is, but you won't know what contributes to the variance or where to begin your improvements. ABM is about solving problems not creating them.

Activity Based Management Solution

You can roll up the expenses and total ABC costs to different levels in the organization similar to the roll-up of expenses and revenues in the General Ledger. The details of ABM can be summarized at each level for management reporting. The summarization enables traceability up and down the organizational chart. For example, assume that ABI's managers for Departments A, B, C, and D all report to the same person in their Business Unit and Departments E and F report to another. Note: we are using the term Business Unit to differentiate this method from the summary departments. Another approach is to summarize departments by process or function. Regardless, the calculation is the same. In this case, the organization chart would look similar to the one below:

Business Unit 1

    Department A
    Department B
    Department C
    Department D

Business Unit 2

    Department E
    Department F

ABI Executives want to hold middle managers responsible for the performance of their groups and direct reports. So, the middle manager would find it helpful to look at both the total expenses and the total ABC cost at the group level. This is done by rolling up the department costs by Business Unit. To show this we will start at the department level with Department B's Department ABC Variance Report shown in Table 8.6.

Department ABC Variance Report

Table 8.6

	Period 1		Period 2		Variance ($)	
Expense Category	Actual Expense	Activity Based Cost	Actual Expense	Activity Based Cost	Period 1	Period 2
Labor	$124,800	$100,000	$100,000	$50,000	$24,800	$50,000
Benefits	$41,600	$33,000	$33,000	$16,500	$8,600	$16,500
Total Personnel:	$166,400	$133,000	$133,000	$66,500	$33,400	$66,500

Table 8.6 (Continued)

Expense Category	Period 1		Period 2		Variance ($)	
	Actual Expense	Activity Based Cost	Actual Expense	Activity Based Cost	Period 1	Period 2
Repairs & Support	$650	$700	$600	$600	($50)	$0
Equipment Depreciation	$3,800	$3,700	$3,000	$2,500	$100	$500
Occupancy	$5,800	$5,550	$5,900	$5,200	$250	$700
Total Property and Equipment:	**$10,250**	**$9,950**	**$9,500**	**$8,300**	**$300**	**$1,200**
Telecommunications	$1,100	$900	$1,100	$1,200	$200	($100)
Outside Services	$100	$75	$50	$50	$25	$0
Legal & Professional	$200	$150	$250	$175	$50	$75
Transportation	$1,200	$900	$1,200	$1,000	$300	$200
Printing & Supplies	$900	$800	$900	$775	$100	$125
Total Other Expenses:	**$3,500**	**$2,825**	**$3,500**	**$3,200**	**$675**	**$300**
Total Expenses:	**$180,150**	**$145,775**	**$146,000**	**$78,000**	**$34,375**	**$68,000**

Next, combine (link) all departments to the Organization Chart, so you can summarize the departments by Business Unit. This summary shows a Business Unit ABC Variance Report. In this example, ABI would roll up Department B (above) with A, C, and D to show the Business Unit 1 Manager how his organization and direct reports are doing. An example of this is shown in Table 8.7.

Table 8.7

	Period 1			Period 2		
	Actual Expenses	Total ABC Cost	Variance	Actual Expenses	Total ABC Cost	Variance
Dept A	$200,000	$180,000	$20,000	$190,000	$170,000	$20,000
Dept B	$180,150	$145,775	$34,375	$146,000	$78,000	$68,000
Dept C	$35,500	$30,000	$5,500	$34,000	$25,000	$9,000
Dept D	$215,000	$205,000	$10,000	$210,000	$205,000	$5,000
Total:	$630,650	$560,775	$69,875	$580,000	$478,000	$102,000

Using this example, the Business Unit 1 manager wants to explain why there is $102,000 in total variance for time-period 2. Using ABM, the manager can see that Department B accounts for 70% of the variance. Researching the variance is easy since this report is simply a summary (roll-up) of the all the department ABC Variance Reports. This method of summarization allows the Business Unit Manager to drill down to see what makes up the variance.

Since ABI used the Resource Costing Methodology, the result is the Department ABC Variance Report shown in Table 8.6. Of course, looking at the Department ABC Variance Report for Department B (Table 8.6), he finds that the variance is due to Personnel (increasing from $33,400 variance in time period 1 to $66,500 in time period 2).

An increase in variance, like that above, often reflects an increase in idle capacity. The Business Unit manager must now look ahead and strategize with the Department B manager. If they identify this as a long-term trend they will need to look at losses through attrition, transferring/loaning people to other areas, *etc.* However, if they are unsure or believe it to be short-term blip, then they may prefer to utilize the extra time for training, process improvements, quality improvements, or other activities to enhance the department's capabilities. In short, the idle time should not be squandered.

FINDING MORE HELP—USING CONSULTANTS

Great consultants can look at an operation and present ideas of how other companies are doing it better or differently. This is like a one-person Benchmarking team. Consultants can also be good facilitators if the company is taking on a new, far-reaching initiative such as Kaizen or Six Sigma. Consultants can also be used to provide some technical expertise or training during new system implementations. However, leaders must transfer as much of that knowledge to their own employees as possible. Knowledge transfer will prevent a knowledge drain (brain drain) when the consultant leaves.

Tip:

A word of caution. Beware of "cost cutting" recommendations. Cost cutting only treats the symptoms. It is a shortsighted, band-aid approach to long-term systemic problems.

The best way to find good consultants is by word of mouth. Talk to others in your industry or company. Find out which consultants were the most helpful and whose advice proved valuable. Second, set firm measurable objectives. Define ahead of time what you want done, what the end-result should look like, and exactly what part of that result you expect from the consultant. Consultants will often write these objectives up as part of their documentation as a Statement of Work and present it back to you for your approval. This presentation is a key ingredient of any successful project since it ensures the consultant has understood your needs and is focused on the right tasks. Finally, remember there are always alternatives. Several of these alternatives are described below.

Alternative # 1: Train and develop your internal Activity Based Management Team. These people should be your best and brightest folks. Process improvement experience, good people skills, and the ability to learn new technologies quickly (since most of the services industry is based on information technology) are the essential traits. Challenge them to come up with process improvement, continuous improvement, and resource utilization analyses that create long-term solutions to systematic problems.

Alternative #2: Many companies have Internal Facilitators attached to their training, Project Management or Human Resources departments. These folks are very skilled at facilitating meetings, organizing projects, and developing timelines/documentation for projects. Using Internal Facilitators is often less expensive and has the added benefit of leveraging the expertise you already have in house. Good leaders from other departments or facilities can also be tapped as facilitators or to provide "outside of the box" ideas. It is always a good idea to develop and utilize the talent you already have. As the old adage says "If you cut your own wood, it shall warm you twice". You should utilize your own talent internally both as a development path and to ensure that the knowledge and expertise remains within the firm after the project is completed.

Alternative #3: <u>Conduct your own benchmarking.</u> Benchmarking can be done both internally and externally. There are many creative ways to find and use benchmarking partners. See the Benchmarking section for more details.

Alternative #4: <u>Hire on Contingency.</u> This approach is seldom used with consulting agencies. In Hire on Contingency, consultants are only paid for what improvements are actually implemented and only after completion of the improvements. Think of this as profit sharing. Obviously, most consulting firms won't like this. But remind them that you are not paying for advice. You are paying for solutions. No solutions implemented, no payment made. This arrangement shows their professionalism and a level of confidence in their own abilities to find the best solutions for your problems.

PROCESS IMPROVEMENT TECHNIQUES

The techniques presented in this section will provide you with a brief overview of several of the most popular Improvement Techniques. This section is not intended to make you an expert on any of these. Instead, it is intended to give you a brief overview of each technique and whet your appetite for more knowledge. Each technique has been the subject of many books on its own.

Remember that this is not an all-inclusive list. New techniques are being developed every day and new technologies are frequently developed to support the techniques. The important point is that all these tools, when used properly, will work. Think of them as tools in a tool belt. You need to understand when to use each one. You use a hammer to drive a nail and a screwdriver to turn a screw, not the other way around. Process improvement techniques work the same way. Each tool can have a big impact when used correctly. Read this section, and then do more research on the techniques you find most interesting.

Process Improvements in Sales or Other Overhead Departments (SG&A)

Processes for Sales, Finance, Accounting, Human Resources, and other overhead functions can be improved. Each function may have different problems and issues, but the approach to finding improvement opportunities will often be the same. The important thing is to hold managers accountable for making improvements. Accountability can be attained by setting and reinforcing expectations. Set the expectations that expenses must decrease while maintaining or improving the level of service.

One way successful organizations hold SG&A managers accountable for costs is to set a goal of decreasing year over year expenses by a specified percent. Another option is keeping the budget flat year over year for several years. However, several conditions should be placed on any such goals:

1. Headcount reduction must be the direct result of legitimate Processes Improvement, not "cost cutting".

2. The total year's expenses must be decreased by X%.

3. Resources and training must be made available to assist in the improvements.

4. Managers and Executives must be motivated to take action. Bonuses and incentive payments etc. should depend on the long-term results of the improvement.

The first point has been explained earlier in this book. The intention of the decrease in expenses is process improvement, not cost cutting. So, headcount reductions, if necessary, must be the result of real process improvements not "cost cutting" initiatives.

Decreasing the total year's expenses forces managers to take immediate steps and seek out process improvements. The longer a manager takes to find improvements the harder it will be to achieve the 5% for the year. For example, if a department has expenses of $100,000 and the goal is 5%, then the manager must save a total of $5,000 by year-end. This can be done early in the year by creatively improving a process and saving a mere $417 per month. Or if the manager waits until September to make the change then the he must be able to improve by $1,250 per month in order to meet the 5% ($5,000) requirement. This is affectionately called "The Squeeze". The longer a manager waits to take action the tougher it will be to make the number.

Adequate resources must also be provided to enable managers to accomplish the improvements and superior achievement must be rewarded. You must make sure the tools and support necessary are available and in sufficient quantities to allow leaders to succeed. Often this will require employee training, new software systems, upgrades *etc.* Brainstorm what will be needed and scope the project accordingly. Also, remember that ideas for improvement can come from anywhere. The most important thing is to <u>Take Action!</u>

Make it fun. Make a "gentleman's wager" between the Business Units to see who can make the largest % improvement. Then set leaders loose and see what they can do. You can give away fun prizes to the winner and/or hold them accountable by linking bonuses/incentives to the improvement goals.

Regardless of whether you use these ideas to champion your change, the need still exists to improve SG&A areas. The techniques that work most efficiently for these areas are Benchmarking, Surveys, and Reengineering. These can be done in tandem or separately and each will be discussed in the sections below.

Surveys

Surveys were discussed earlier in the book. As a result, we will only review a few of the finer points here. Table 5.2 shows the results of a sample survey. As mentioned earlier, surveys are a fast and easy way to see where time is spent. They are good for identifying opportunities for improvement and work well for SG&A and overhead departments.

If you can create systematic fixes to a few of the opportunities identified in a survey, you'll buy a lot of votes from the Business Units. The reason is that their incentives are not based on the number of fires they put out, but on how profitable their customers and Products are. So fixing systematic issues will save them a lot of stress and help them focus on improving profitability. Likewise, an increase in revenue (sales) is more likely to improve the profitability of a corporation faster than an increase in the number of fires extinguished.

Avoid doing surveys in a group setting. First, it is hard to get two or more people to agree on the percentage of time spent. People spend their time in different ways, support different Products or customers, and each person has different strengths and weaknesses. Second, in larger groups, the loudest voice sometimes has the greatest weight. But this doesn't necessarily mean they have the best process, ideas, or experience. It just means they express themselves more vocally than others do. So, be careful about doing surveys in a group setting.

Surveys are also done better face to face. This is especially true with Sales Teams. Sales folks spend so much time on the road that it is hard to get in contact with them and to get them to complete the survey on a timely basis. It is often easier to set a firm time to meet with them or grab them on their way through the office. A convenient time to meet with people is often first thing in the morning, or right after another meeting.

Conducting surveys face to face also affords the opportunity for the participant to ask questions and for the Activity Based Management Team to clarify some of the survey items. This technique allows the team to gain perspective, increase buy-in, and ensure the questions are interpreted consistently. If you can't get to each employee, try the manager. Often the manager is very experienced, has a good idea of how everything is done, and knows what the aggravation points or speed bumps are in the area.

Process Reengineering

Michael Hammer and James Champy popularized process Reengineering with the book Reengineering the Corporation. Reengineering emphasizes taking a fresh, holistic view of how organizations should operate. This fresh look is done without regard to how the organization currently operates. Reengineering involves breaking apart the activities in an organization (without regard to any processes currently in place) and then building them back up into a better process.

One way to facilitate Reengineering is the Yellow Post-It method. You get everyone in a room with several large stacks of yellow Post-It notes for a series of three meetings. In the fist meeting, the facilitator leads the group through a brainstorming exercise. The group randomly lists all the functions or activities performed in the process or group. Each item is written on a Post-It note and stuck to wall. This exercise is very visual and tends to be both energizing and draining. So, keep the meeting to one hour. Continue the brainstorming meeting on another day, if necessary.

The second meeting can be run two different ways. One way is to start putting the post it notes into functional groups with related items. Don't name the groupings yet, just move the Post-It notes around and see how it turns out. This method puts the responsibility for certain functions on one person or team.

The other (preferred) option for the second meeting is to put the Post-It notes in the order in which they should occur. This is called process orientation and is done from your customer's vantage point. The process approach puts responsibility for the whole process from start to finish on one person or team. This creates true ownership of the results. Having it all in one place makes it very easy to find duplications of effort and streamline operations. It also makes it easy for leaders to lead. The whole process approach ensures that one person can manage and supervise the service from start to finish. It decreases the chances of miscommunication, in-fighting, and silo think. One group is responsible for the overall result.

The third meeting provides an opportunity to organize the notes, and give a name to the groupings or processes. The groupings reflect what the workflow should be through the department and highlight areas that might have duplicated efforts. Finally, organize or shift resources around so that people are able to succeed. Again, the goal is to streamline the entire chain of events.

Benchmarking Processes

Benchmarking is an excellent way to gain perspective and find improvement ideas. This can be done internally or externally. Either way, the process is the same. Examine another group's processes and see what they are doing better or differently than you. Look for similarities. Ask yourself why are they doing better? Find out what sets them apart. Then document your findings. The successes and efficient processes found in one group can often be used as a cookie cutter for improving others.

The most powerful way to implement Benchmarking is to visit other (external) organizations that have similar functions. The reason it is so powerful is because you get exposed to fresh ideas. You are not re-hashing the same tired old ideas again and again. External benchmarking provides the greatest opportunity to leap ahead of the competition.

Some people cringe at the idea of benchmarking external groups. You may hear expressions such as:

- "We're unique, no one else does what we do."

- "Our industry is different, the only ones we can Benchmark are our competitors and neither of us would agree to that."

- "We're so far ahead of our competitors that they should be Benchmarking us!"

We could only hope that the last one is true. In reality, technology changes so fast that you can go to bed one night on top of the world, but get blown away by the competition before you arrive at work the next morning. No industry or corporation can afford to sit back on its haunches. This book is about Taking Action and Benchmarking is an excellent way to do this. There are two basic types of Benchmark: Benchmarking Processes and Benchmarking ABC costs. We'll discuss each below.

Benchmarking Processes

Benchmarking Processes is the more traditional and preferred method. First, you determine what function(s) of your business you want to improve. Then brainstorm other industries and businesses that perform the same type of <u>function</u>. Be creative and "think outside of the box". Next, take the list of industries/businesses and ask around. See if anyone knows somebody who works in the other industry. It is likely you know someone who can make an introduction or provide a contact. All you need is a name and a number.

Ask around in your professional organizations. Check with the Chamber of Commerce, the Better Business Bureau, your accountant, or even an outside consultant. Failing that, obtain a list of businesses by looking through your phone book.

Next, call the contact. Explain whom you are, what you are looking for and set a time for a site visit. There is not much to prepare. All your team members have to do is bring a pen, paper, and an open mind. Then at the end of you visit, offer to return the favor for your new Benchmarking partner. The Benchmark process steps are summarized below.

1.   Select a function to Benchmark

2.   Brainstorm other businesses that have a similar function

3.   Find a contact

4.   Set-up a site visit

5.   Improve your processes

6.   Return the favor.

It is that simple. Notice that you should always offer to allow the other company to come to your site for a visit. You should do this out of professional courtesy. More selfishly, you do this because you can learn just as much by hosting a site visit as you can by going on one. So, keep an open mind as you return the favor and see what questions they ask. You may be surprised by how much you can improve your own operation by listening and responding honestly to their questions. Be sure to point out what improvements you've made from your visit to their shop; it is a great compliment.

Who should attend the Benchmarking site visit?

Your team should consist of at least three people: one manager (supervisor or team-lead), one or two energetic employees who are intimately familiar with your process, and an Activity Based Management Tactician as a facilitator. The ABM Team member can offer suggestions about what to look for in your visit, and share experiences from other Benchmarking endeavors. The bottom line is that you want have enough people to brainstorm ideas effectively and be able sell it back to your own organization. But, not so many people that you overwhelm the host.

Who should be Benchmarked?

Ideally you should Benchmark companies who perform a particular function the best. Notice that the best performers are not usually in your industry. You could also narrow the list down to companies in your geographical area; those that you can visit in one day. Your site visit will normally only last a couple of hours so you do not need to spend a lot of money on airfare, hotels, and other travel expenses. Think outside the box. If you can't get the best company, then pick one that's fairly good and conveniently located. Benchmarking is not about mimicking someone else, it is about getting fresh ideas to improve your processes.

For example, assume that ABI wants to Benchmark a Call Center. They could try to look for partners at other banks, but of course they won't find any takers. Instead, they could turn to other industries or banks in other geographic areas. They can look around for airlines, car rental agencies, hotel chains, or other local businesses with Call Centers. Their Products may differ, but the core function is the same; answer the telephone, look up information on the computer system, provide feedback, and make a sale. In this case, ABI settles on a nearby hotel chain's Call Center since it is located in the same town and tends to have very good customer service. It is that simple.

Still not convinced you can find a Benchmarking partner? Look at the table in Appendix C for a sample listing. This is not an all-inclusive list, but it should stimulate some ideas for you.

Benchmarking ABC Costs

Some groups try to Benchmark the costs of an Industry or another corporation. This is difficult to do given the different methods of gathering and summarizing the information. People are also reluctant to reveal their financial information to outsiders. Sometimes third parties try to do this on an anonymous basis. However, the results are seldom worthwhile. For example, the range of values from the minimum to the maximum can be so large, that it's obviously not an "apple-to-apple" comparison.

If you choose to participate in a third party benchmarking project, make sure there are clear guidelines on how the data should be gathered. Make sure you know exactly what should be included in each cost. Also, find out how to present the data to the third party and how it will be presented back as the final product. If data isn't gathered and presented in a consistent way, the benchmarks will be meaningless. You may also be required to pay a fee to the third party, to receive a copy of the Benchmark results.

There are several reasons you may not want to participate in Benchmarking ABC costs. First, seeing the numbers doesn't tell you how to improve. Benchmarked ABC costs only show where you stand in comparison to others, not what is behind the costs. If you are losing or winning a lot of bids for new business, then you probably know this already. Second, if the range between the low and high values in the survey is substantial, then chances are good you are comparing apples to oranges. Lastly, if you were not comfortable with your costs internally (and some people aren't), why would you submit them for others to see? This would make your group look bad and skew the results for others. Because of these concerns, it is preferable to Benchmark Processes, not ABC costs. Besides, Benchmarking Processes is fun, free, and you get many wonderful, "out of the box ideas" on how to improve.

Bottleneck Analysis (Theory of Constraints)

Bottlenecking was popularized in Eli Goldratt's book: *The Goal*. Bottleneck Theory (also called Theory of Constraints or TOC) teaches that the speed, quality, and efficiency of an entire process are only as good as its weakest member. For example, if you have several steps in a process, the slowest one will determine how fast the overall process can flow. Lets say ABI has a process with five steps. The step capacities are 25, 25, 5, 32, and 31 items per hour respectively. Running the processes at full speed will result in the actual throughput per hour as shown in Table 8.8.

Table 8.8

	Capability	Actual Throughput
Step 1	25	25
Step 2	25	25
Step 3	5	5
Step 4	32	5
Step 5	31	5

The bottleneck (constraint) on the overall process is Step 3 as shown in Table 8.8 above. Its capability is 5, which is the limiting factor in the overall process. It doesn't matter how fast Steps 1, 2, 4, or 5 go, the maximum the overall all process can produce in any given hour is 5.

In this case, one of two scenarios will occur. One, the employees at Step 1 and Step 2 may continue performing 25 transactions per hour. This action will cause a backlog of work waiting on step 3. Table 8.9 illustrates this scenario.

Step 3 Servicing Volumes

Table 8.9

	Beginning Queue	Added to Queue (from Step 2)	Actual Throughput	Ending Queue
Hour 2	0	25	5	20
Hour 3	20	25	5	40
Hour 4	40	25	5	60
Hour 5	60	25	5	80
Hour 6	80	25	5	100
		Avg Throughput:	5	

As shown in Table 8.9 the average throughput for Step 3 is five items per hour. Whereas the number of items completed from Step 2 is 25 per hour. This means the queue (transactions waiting for Step 3) continues to grow at a rate of

20 (25 - 5) additional items per hour. This will continue until the backlog and inventory build-up becomes unmanageable.

The second, more likely, scenario is that ABI will put a band-aid solution on Step 3. They may do this by having the employees in Steps 1, 2, 4, and 5 work on other items until Step 3 is ready for more work. Alternatively, they might add more people to Step 3 or have the other employees help with Step 3. These are shortsighted solutions and only treat the symptoms the process. These actions cover up the inefficiencies of Step 3. The real problem according to bottlenecking and the Theory of Constraints is that Step 3 is too slow. Step 3 is the bottleneck and it should be improved until it is no longer the constraint or until it can produce at the minimum level demanded.

Another way to look at this is in terms how often a completed transaction will be produced. If the slowest step in a process takes 3 minutes, then one transaction will be completed, on average, every 3 minutes. The 3-minute step is the bottleneck/constraint. So to improve the overall process (decrease the average transaction completion time) you must improve the 3-minute step. You keep improving that step until it is no longer the slowest step, at which point some other part becomes the constraint. Then you work on the next constraint until it, too, is no longer the constraint, *etc.* You continue this until you reach the desired production rate.

Tip:

Set your goal ahead of time. Figure out how many items need to be produced per hour or per day to meet your demand. Then improve your constraints until they reach your goal. Unsure of your desired demand? Look at your actual production history, budgeted production volume and any seasonality factors or expected market fluctuations. These factors should lead you to a fair number.

Spotting Bottlenecks

There are several ways to spot a bottleneck. First, you can look at the activity times from the time studies. These should be readily available in your ABM system. Another way is graph the capabilities versus the actual throughputs as shown in Figure 8.5.

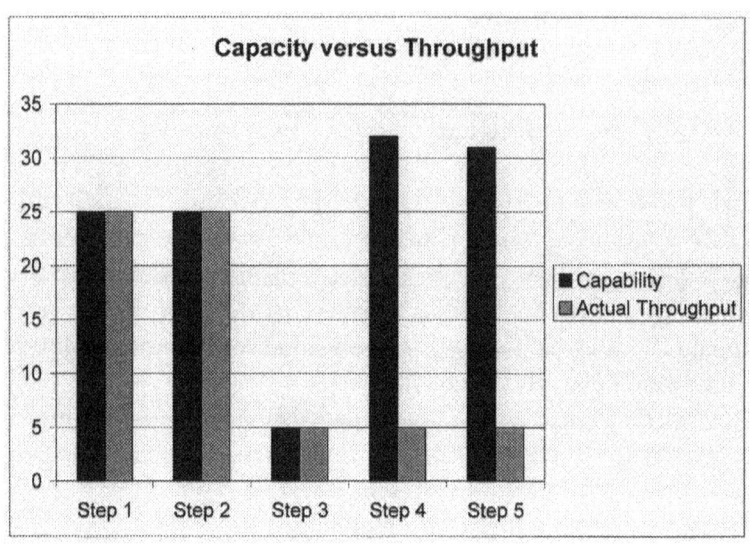

Figure 8.5

You can also study the process flow charts and maps based on your activity times and Product Life Cycles. Or you can spend a couple hours in the Gemba (where the work is performed). Just grab a chair and sit out in the middle of the action. Go ahead. People will think you are nuts. But, watch to see how people are moving and where the work is piling up. Look to see who is waiting on a prior step to be completed before the next can begin. These are indications of bottle-necks or some other malady plaguing the area. Just sit and watch. Before long, these and other items will jump out at you and scream: "Fix me! Fix me!" Then all you have to do is Take Action.

Next, as mentioned before, process improvements for the sake of improvement itself, add little value to the organization. There must be a positive impact on the financials or customer satisfaction to make it meaningful. This improvement may be seen as a decrease in actual expenses, an increase in quality/customer satisfaction, an increase in sales, or an increase in the actual throughput of your process (and thereby increasing the sales). Use your ABM system to monitor your improvements and keep it up to date to better track capacity.

Many people mistakenly perform process improvements to increase capacity. If your goal is to have more capacity then you've accomplished it. Well done! But have you really accomplished anything? If your goal is to increase your revenues then you must increase <u>and</u> utilize the capacity. TOC is not about increasing the capability (the amount of items that <u>can go</u> through a process). It is about increasing the number of items that actually <u>DO</u> go through the process and get sold. This is what we mean by increasing throughput.

Don't take this to mean that increasing capacity is bad. It's not. You just have to do it for the right reasons. Increasing capacity is a good idea when the department or process is over capacity and bursting at the seams. It may also be appropriate to study the capacity when you find a bottleneck and need to reduce it for the organization to gain market share or profitability. In short, make sure the improvement helps the bottom line.

Six Sigma

Six Sigma is another improvement technique that originated in manufacturing. It is a wonderful, systematic way to improve highly repetitive processes. It is a straightforward logical method used to identify problems and customer requirements. You can then work backwards to improve the process until it meets those requirements or fixes the problem. Six Sigma has worked well in many organizations and contains many tools and techniques to aid you in your endeavors. It does require training and must have the ardent support of upper management. So, do your homework and make sure you understand how Six Sigma works.

Six Sigma is often misunderstood as a quality improvement technique. Six Sigma actually refers to the process of improvement and the tools you use to accomplish this. One way to use these tools is for quality improvement. For example, you can use its systematic approach to analyze a process, identify variations, and track down root causes. You then eliminate the variations, which results in a more consistent quality. Therefore, improved quality and increased customer satisfaction are the results of the technique not the technique itself.

Additionally, process variances cause inefficiencies in your process. Inefficiencies waste valuable time. Time that could be used for production, increased quality, or process improvement. Traditionally, people build additional systems and processes to work around the problems, adding more quality checks, or performing rework on items, *etc*. This just covers up the problems. Eliminating the variations standardizes the process and creates greater opportunities for improvement.

Through Six Sigma, you can design experiments to find the causes of the variations, and recommend/justify improvements. It helps you to make your processes capable of getting the same result every time. Since this kind of analysis involves the use of statistics, experimental design, and some data crunching, it is not for the faint of heart. There are occasions, however, when this grunt work is necessary and valuable.

Too often, the Six Sigma Teams go out and make a lot of "improvements" without understanding how they affect the bottom line or how to manage from the improvements (see discussion on improving idle capacity). This is where ABM comes into play. Your ABM system needs to be in place to get your organization acclimated to managing based on the costs and resources available before embarking on a Six Sigma program. The information in your system will be of great assistance when validating Six Sigma improvements. The ABM data will need to be updated continuously to reflect any improvement efforts.

You also need the right mix of talent in place to be able to learn Six Sigma and use it to improve your organization. Remember, Six Sigma is not a quick fix. It may take several years before <u>sustained</u> improvement can be quantified and validated.

Tip:

For research and development or software development teams, Six Sigma may be too confining. Alternative methods might include SEI (Software Engineering Institute), Lean or some other improvement program.

In short, Six Sigma and ABM complement one another. ABM identifies the work areas requiring improvement and reflects the improvements in the activity time, ABC cost, and profitability reports. Six Sigma digs into the details, tracks down root causes, and eliminates process variances. Using these two tools, together, can be a powerful combination.

Value Added Analysis

Another popular way to look for improvements is by classifying functions and processes as Value Added or Non-Value Added. Value Added functions are tasks that the customer is willing to pay for. Non-Value Added functions are those that are of no interest to the customer and he would not be willing to pay for. You can identify these as part of your Process Mapping and Activity Based Costing. An example of Value Added analysis is shown below:

Process: Return Item to Customer

Function	Value Added?	Reason
Receive request to return item	Yes	Required to return the item
Retrieve item	Yes	Required to return the item
Copy request and item	No	Customer isn't requesting that you keep a copy of it.
File Copy of request and item at desk	No	Customer doesn't care if you file a copy of the request or not.
Package item, address and send to customer	Yes	Required to return the item

In this example, an employee is keeping a copy of the item and request at their desk as a record of what was sent. This function may be done for several reasons:

1. To record how many requests were made.

2. To be used in case there are any follow up questions about the request, or

3. Because that's the way it has always been done.

The time it takes to walk to the copy machine, copy it, and file the copy at the employee's desk is non-value added time (wasted time). Sometimes the copy machine is broken and the employee has to fix it…wasted time. If the employee can't fix it and service has to be called, then it may delay the employee in sending the item to customer. More wasted time. You get the idea. The wasted time and the cost of paper utilized for the copier is non-value added and should be eliminated.

Some Non-Value Added functions are required for business purposes or for regulatory reasons. For this reason some people with break functions into three groups, Value Added, Business Requirement (includes regulatory), and Non-Value Added. Again, all Non-Value Added functions should be questioned and eliminated whenever possible. Business Requirements should be combined or automated whenever possible to minimize their cost on the organization's resources.

Performing Value Added Analyses may cause you to ask if an activity should be done at all. Or is it possible for the customer to do it through the Internet, an automated phone line, or some other automated system? These are all good questions and the type of thought provoking outcomes you can expect from Value Added Analysis.

Lean Servicing/Lean Operations

Lean Operations can also be called Lean Manufacturing or Lean Servicing depending on what type of company or area you work in. Lean is a philosophy more than a process improvement technique. It is a state to aspire to rather than a way to get there. Becoming a Lean Organization means that you are eliminating waste, removing bottlenecks, and enabling the organization to run as efficiently as possible.

Lean is not a goal. Goals are quantifiable and achievable. It is very difficult to achieve a philosophy (Lean). Therefore, Lean is better used as a vision or a value for a corporation. To follow the vision of becoming a "Lean Organization" you could set goals for ROE, expense Reduction, throughput increase, revenue increase, *etc*. All of which are measurable, quantifiable, attainable results.

A company, which aspires to be "Lean" and utilize "Lean Thinking", analyzes its processes and looks for ways to improve. Such a company analyzes its ABC costs and expects that improving those and eliminating unnecessary activities will allow it to become a more efficient organization. Efficiency improvements can be done using one or more of the techniques described above (Benchmarking, Bottlenecking, Six Sigma, Value Added Analyses etc.). You can also do this through quality initiatives such as TQM (Total Quality Management), ISO or QS since these techniques seek to eliminate defects and ensure a more consistent result. Regardless, ABM plays a crucial role in monitoring and reporting improvements. The accumulation of these improvements over time will improve the company's metrics and financial goals.

Conclusion

CHECKING THE RESULTS

ABCs of Activity Based Management covered a lot of information. We walked step by step through setting up the ABM system, gathering activity times, calculating costs, reporting, and improvement techniques. The only thing we haven't covered is how to check the results. In other words, how do you know if your improvements have made a difference?

This first indication is the smile on the manager's face and congratulatory handshake for a job well done. Beyond that, it is all in the numbers. No process improvement is truly successful unless the profitability improves. Profitability improvement is accomplished by either increasing revenues (throughput) or by decreasing the actual expenses. In the end, the accumulation of many successful process improvements will be an increase in the company's ROE, ROA or any other measure you used to set your goals. Each measure can be seen on the company's quarterly and annual financial reports. Showing success in the short term is also very easy. List the departments that were improved and compare their expenses, revenues or metrics before and after. An example is shown below.

	Expenses			
	Before	**After**	**$ Savings**	**% Change**
Department A	$250,000	$175,000	$75,000	30%
Department B	$155,000	$133,000	$22,000	14%
Department C	$345,000	$243,000	$102,000	30%
Total	**$750,000**	**$551,000**	**$199,000**	**27%**

The table above shows that the team achieved overall savings of $199,000. The numbers presented are actually the average expenses for the three months prior and the three months after the process improvements. You don't want to use just one period for computing your savings. One month does not constitute a trend. The report above should be done using a three-month average then again one year later using a year over year comparison. If you are still seeing significant savings after one year, you can feel very good that you've made a lasting impact on the company's profitability.

The quarterly and annual financial reports only show results in aggregate. You can't see the details about where progress is being made. The great thing about ABM is that you can and do have that information. You can see improvements by department, Product, service or customer and it is at your fingertips.

The same type of analysis can be done at a higher level in the company (i.e. Business Unit). A high level analysis would prove that the expenses were actually improved, not shifted from one area to another. This analysis can also be done for Product profitability and customer portfolio profitability. Looking at the results by Product and customer portfolio will again ensure that the expenses and throughput were actually improved, and that they were not offset by increases the idle capacity or SG&A costs. In the long run, this comparison should be done with each of your metrics (ROE, ROA etc.). Then, publicize your successes and keep the momentum going.

SUMMARY

This book discussed many topics and presented a large amount of information on how to design, implement, and utilize Activity Based Management. As you progress in your ABM efforts, it will be necessary to explain this concept to others in easy to understand language. One way that has works well is to use the acronym CPI. CPI stands for:

1. Cost by Function (Activity)

2. Profitability by Account

3. Improve by Process

Cost by Function—Develop your costs by function or activity. This is commonly referred to as Activity Based Costing. This information feeds the cost side of profitability.

Profitability by Account—Transaction profitability at the account level can be summarized, analyzed, and reported in any way you desire. These reports can then be used to manage and improve your business by improving operations (ABM Variance Report), customer, Product, and channel profitability.

Improve by Process—Don't simply improve some of the detailed steps or activities involved in a transaction. Seek improvement for the overall process and all departments that have an impact on that transaction. Total process improvement is the only way to take huge leaps ahead, minimize hand-offs, achieve efficiencies, and improve profitability across the whole company.

AUTHOR'S NOTE

I hope this book has proven as satisfying for you to read, as it was for me to write. Remember, the results of any technique you elect to pursue (Activity Based Management, Six Sigma, *etc.*) will only be as good as the leaders and teams who use them. Select talented folks, provide a clear vision of how you want things to run, then set them loose and let them achieve. I wish you the best of luck in achieving your goals and anything else you set out to do.

R. William Frost
rnlfrst@netscape.net

APPENDIX A

Sample Cost Driver List

Cost Driver	Unit of Measure	Cost Driver Definition	Data Source
Cash a Customer Check—Branch	# of Occurrences	Cost per occurrence of cashing a check at a Branch Office	Teller System
Cash-in Certificate of Deposit	# of Occurrences	Cost per occurrence of a customer cashing (redeeming) a Certificate of Deposit	Deposit Account System
Cash-in Savings Bond	# of Occurrences	Cost per occurrence of a customer cashing (redeeming) a Savings Bond	Deposit Account System
Cash Withdrawal—ATM	# of Occurrences	Cost per occurrence of withdrawing cash from an Automated Teller Machine	Automated Teller System
Cash Withdrawal—Branch	# of Occurrences	Cost per occurrence of withdrawing cash at a Branch Office	Teller System
Close an Account—Branch	# of Occurrences	Cost per occurrence of closing an account through a Branch Office	Deposit Account System
Close an Account—Call Center	# of Occurrences	Cost per occurrence of closing an account through Call Center	Call Center System

Cost Driver	Unit of Measure	Cost Driver Definition	Data Source
Close an Account—Internet	# of Occurrences	Cost per occurrence of closing an account through internet	Internet System
Initiate a Check Order—Call Center	# of Occurrences	Cost per occurrence of processing a check order request through Call Center	Call Center System
Initiate a Check Order—Internet	# of Occurrences	Cost per occurrence of processing a check order request through internet	Internet System
Initiate a Customer Statement	# of Occurrences	Cost per occurrence of preparing and mailing a customer statement	Deposit Account System
Initiate a Deposit—Branch	# of Items	Cost per item of processing a customer deposit through a Branch Office	Teller System
Initiate a Deposit—Cash Vault	# of Items	Cost per item for processing a customer deposit in the Cash Vault	Deposit Account System
Initiate a Deposit—Off-Site ATM	# of Items	Cost per item for processing a deposit at an off-site Automated Teller Machine (Courier)	Teller System
Initiate a Deposit—On-Site ATM	# of Items	Cost per item for processing an deposit at an on-site Automated Teller Machine (Branch Office)	Teller System
Initiate a Payment—ATM	# of Occurrences	Cost per occurrence of processing a payment initiated through an Automated Teller Machine	Automated Teller System
Initiate a Payment—Branch	# of Occurrences	Cost per occurrence of processing a payment initiated through a Branch Office	Teller System

Cost Driver	Unit of Measure	Cost Driver Definition	Data Source
Initiate a Payment—Call Center	# of Occurrences	Cost per occurrence of processing a payment initiated through Call Center	Loan System
Initiate a Payment—Internet	# of Occurrences	Cost per occurrence of processing a payment initiated through internet	Loan System
Initiate a POS Transaction	# of Transactions	Cost per transaction for Debit Card purchases (Point of Sale)	Automated Teller System
Initiate a Stop Payment—Branch	# of Items	Cost per item of placing a stop pay at a Branch Office	Deposit Account System
Initiate a Stop Payment—Call Center	# of Items	Cost per item of placing a stop pay through Call Center	Call Center System
Initiate a Stop Payment—Internet	# of Items	Cost per item of placing a stop pay through internet	Internet System
Initiate a Transfer—ATM	# of Occurrences	Cost per occurrence of processing an account transfer initiated through an Automated Teller Machine	Automated Teller System
Initiate a Transfer—Branch	# of Occurrences	Cost per occurrence of transferring funds initiated through a Branch Office	Teller System
Initiate a Transfer—Call Center	# of Occurrences	Cost per occurrence of transferring funds initiated through Call Center	Call Center System
Initiate a Transfer—Internet	# of Occurrences	Cost per occurrence of transferring funds initiated through the internet	Internet System
Initiate a Wire Transaction	# of Occurrences	Cost per occurrence of transferring funds using the wire transfer system	Wire Transfer System

Cost Driver	Unit of Measure	Cost Driver Definition	Data Source
Initiate an Balance Inquiry—ATM	# of Occurrences	Cost per occurrence of a balance inquiry through an Automated Teller Machine	Automated Teller System
Initiate an Balance Inquiry—Branch	# of Occurrences	Cost per occurrence of a balance inquiry through a Branch Office	Teller System
Initiate an Balance Inquiry—Call Center	# of Occurrences	Cost per occurrence of a balance inquiry through Call Center	Call Center System
Initiate an Balance Inquiry—Internet	# of Occurrences	Cost per occurrence of a balance inquiry through the internet	Internet System
Initiate an ACH Transaction	# of Occurrences	Cost per occurrence of electronically moving funds into/out of a bank account	Automated Clearing House System
Initiate an Advance—ATM	# of Occurrences	Cost per occurrence of processing an advance through an Automated Teller Machine	Automated Teller System
Initiate an Advance—Branch	# of Occurrences	Cost per occurrence of processing an advance through a Branch Office	Teller System
Initiate an Overdraft Transaction	# of Occurrences	Cost per occurrence of processing an item through an account with insufficient funds	Deposit Account System
Open a Customer Account—Branch	# of Occurrences	Cost per occurrence of opening an account through a Branch Office	Deposit Account System
Open a Customer Account—Call Center	# of Occurrences	Cost per occurrence of opening an account through Call Center	Call Center System

Cost Driver	Unit of Measure	Cost Driver Definition	Data Source
Open a Customer Account—Internet	# of Occurrences	Cost per occurrence of opening an account through the internet	Internet System
Update Customer Informa- tion—Branch	# of Accounts	Periodic customer account updates, problem resolu- tion, financial reviews *etc.* through a Branch Office	Deposit Account System
Update Customer Information—Call Center	# of Accounts	Periodic customer account updates, problem resolu- tion, financial reviews *etc.* through the Call Center	Call Center Sys- tem
Update Customer Informa- tion—Internet	# of Accounts	Periodic customer account updates, problem resolu- tion, financial reviews *etc.* through the internet	Internet System

APPENDIX B

Sample Fixed and Variable Costs

Fixed Costs
Labor—Exempt
Benefits—Exempt
Other Personnel Expense (Tuition Reimbursement, Recruiting, Relocation etc.)
Repairs & Maintenance
Depreciation
Occupancy (Facilities, Real Estate Taxes, Utilities etc.)
Other Leases
Telecommunications
Legal & Professional
Marketing & Advertising
Travel & Entertainment

Variable Costs
Labor—Non-Exempt
Bonuses
Overtime
Commissions
Temporary or Contract Help
Benefits—Non-Exempt

Variable Costs
Transportation
Printing & Supplies
Postage
Credit Reports
Outside Services

APPENDIX C

Benchmarking Partners

Function or Process	Potential Partners
Call centers	Banks, hotel chains, airlines, car rental agencies, travel agencies, insurance companies, HMOs, *etc.*
On-Line (internet) service for account support and basic transactions	Banks, hotel chains, airlines, car rental agencies, travel agencies, insurance companies, HMOs, manufacturers (EDI), on-line retailers, *etc.*
Automated processing and imaging	Banks, insurance companies, automated manufacturing cells, charge card companies, United States Postal Service, UPS, FedEx
Automated Clearing House/wires	On-line retailers, web hosting companies, on-line auction companies, *etc.*
Customer queues and wait times	Fast food restaurants, video rental stores, movie theatres, amusement parks, *etc.*
Leading process improvement	Manufacturers (Six Sigma, Lean Manufacturing, Kanban, Continuous Improvement, TQM, *etc.*), consulting agencies
Human Resources	Banks, hotel chains, airlines, car rental agencies, travel agencies, insurance companies, HMOs, manufacturers, retail stores, hospitals—i.e. virtually any corporation

Function or Process	Potential Partners
Information/technical services	Banks, hotel chains, airlines, car rental agencies, travel agencies, insurance companies, HMOs, manufacturers, retail stores, hospitals—i.e. virtually any corporation
Change Management	Any company that recently (successfully) installed a new enterprise or business intelligence system.
Building services, building maintenance, equipment maintenance	Manufacturing, banks, hotel chains, airlines, car rental agencies, travel agencies, insurance companies, HMOs, retail stores, trucking companies, warehouses, etc.—i.e. virtually any corporation
Occupancy	Hotels, apartment complexes, hospitals, car dealerships etc.
Unused/idle capacity	Banks, hotel chains, airlines, car rental agencies, travel agencies, insurance companies, HMOs, manufacturers, retail stores, hospitals, Car Dealerships—i.e. virtually any corporation
Regulatory compliance	Banks, insurance companies, airlines, HMOs, hospitals, military, transportation companies etc.
Transportation and internal routing	Federal Express, UPS, United States Post Office, airports (baggage handling), hospitals (patients and records).
Records, statements and customer billing	Hospitals, HMOs, dental offices, insurance companies, banks
Retail inventory management	Bookstores, supermarket stores, discount retailers, warehouse stores (Home Depot, Lowe's, Wal-Mart), car dealerships

APPENDIX D

Responsibilities for Activity Based Management

The matrix below summarizes several of the key players in process improvement and Activity Based Management. Samples of the Reports listed here can be found in the main text. Notice that each level of the organization has a role to play. Senior Executives and Activity Based Management Teams merely facilitate the improvements. Middle Management, Sales Executives, Product Managers, and Department Managers actually make the decisions, manage the improvements, and execute the strategy.

Senior Executives	• Set expectations and goals
	• Lead organizations through change
	• Publicize and recognize successes
	• Reward behaviors and actions that achieve company benchmarks
Middle Management	• Carry out the strategies of ABM and process improvement
	• Facilitate goal achievement by managing expectations and ensuring targets are met or surpassed
	• Provide training and resources for employees to achieve the goals
	• Manage idle capacity—*Idle Capacity Reports*

Sales Executives	• Drive revenues through sales
	• Cross sell profitable Product Lines
	• Ensure customer/portfolio profitability—*Portfolio Profitability and Customer Profitability Reports*
Product Line Managers	• Recommend pricing standards and initiate new Product launches or other means to gain more revenue and market share
	• Ensure Product profitability—*Product Profitability, Bottom Line Contribution and Profit Matrix Reports*
	• Seek out process improvements—*ABC Cost Breakdown Report*
Departmental Managers	• Improve processes by increasing quality, increasing throughput, minimizing aggravation points, and decreasing costs
	• Manage costs and capacity—*Activity Based Management Report*
Activity Based Management Team	• Monitor and maintain ABC costs—*Organizational ABC Variance, Department ABC Variance, ABC Aging, and Product Profitability Reports*
	• Lead organization through process improvements setting sights on items that impact the bottom line, improve quality, eliminate aggravation points, and increase throughput—*ABC Cost Breakdown, Idle Capacity, and SG&A Reports*

APPENDIX E

Selecting an ABC Program

Today there are many pre-packaged software programs to help you conduct time studies, calculate ABC costs, and summarize ABC data for use in Activity Based Management. Some of these packages are expensive, so it is important to select the right one for your needs. The best way to do this is to evaluate software packages the same way you would evaluate a new computer. Make a list of all the features you want. Decide what features are most important ("Must Have"), and which features would be convenient ("Nice to Have"). Then list them in descending order of importance. A sample list is shown below.

Feature	Relative Importance	Software Vendor #1	Software Vendor #2	Software Vendor #3
Calculates Fixed ABC Cost	Must Have	1	1	1
Calculates Variable ABC Cost	Must Have	1	1	1
Calculates Total ABC Cost	Must Have	1	1	1
Export Results to Excel, text file, *etc.* for more detailed analyses	Must Have	1	1	1
Imports List of Products	Must Have	1		1
Imports List of Cost Drivers	Must Have	1		1
Imports Volumes	Must Have	1		1
Imports Expense Lines (Labor, *etc.*)	Must Have	1		1
Imports Activity Times	Must Have	1		1
Service/support contract	Must Have	1		1
Total "Must Have"		**10**	**4**	**10**

Feature	Relative Importance	Software Vendor #1	Software Vendor #2	Software Vendor #3
Open data source (external reporting software can be used to create reports)	Nice to Have	1		1
Customizable reports	Nice to Have	1		
Produces Flow Charts	Nice to Have	1		1
ABC Cost Breakdown Report	Nice to Have		1	
Results accessible via internet/ intranet	Nice to Have		1	
Links easily to existing company systems	Nice to Have	1	1	
Can be used for Product, customer, channel profitability	Nice to Have	1		
Includes statistical, Six Sigma, Lean, or Value Added package	Nice to Have			
Total "Nice to Have"		**5**	**3**	**2**
Total Score		**15**	**7**	**12**

Your list of features may vary depending on what type of software you are looking for and what your needs are. In this example, both the first and third vendors contain all the "Must Have" features. Their totals are shaded grey since they are a "Go" in those areas. Vendor #2 did not meet all the "Must Have" criteria so it not highlighted. Vendor #2's total score is also not shaded since it didn't meet the minimum requirements.

In the "Nice to Have" category, Vendor #1 is shaded grey again since it has the greatest number of bells and whistles. Vendors #2 and #3 are not highlighted since they each contain some of the "Nice to Have" features, but not the most. Thus, with a total score of 15, Vendor #1 is the desired software package. Vendor #3's total score is acceptable since it fulfills all the "Must Have" features. However, it doesn't have greatest number of "Nice to Have" items. Vendor #2s total score is unacceptable because it doesn't meet all the minimum "Must Have" features.

The final step is to compare prices. Both Vendors #1 and #3 meet the minimum criteria, and have open data sources with data extract capability. The "Nice to Have" features that were lacking in either one can be done using external reporting software. Thus, either vendor's software might be suitable for ABI's needs. The deciding factor would then be price. If Vendor #3's price is significantly lower than Vendor #1, then that is the software ABI should purchase. Alternatively, if the prices are similar between the two vendors, then ABI will choose Vendor #1 since it has the higher total score. In either case, ABI's purchasing department will attempt to negotiate the net purchase price down as far as possible.

Other variations on this example involve weighting each of the features for their relative value and including some sort of Return on Investment calculation. Return on Investment is an important factor to consider when deciding whether or not to purchase new software (especially if the difference could have a measurable affect on depreciation or taxes). However, being able to compare the relative timesavings between specific software packages may be difficult. The reason is that you may not actually know which software is faster. You also may not know which is easier without physically loading and testing each one for a period, under actual time study conditions. Thus, Return on Investment was not included in the example above when comparing the vendors.

APPENDIX F

Common Causes of ABC Variance

The table below shows a list of the most common symptoms of ABC Variance (first column). The second column shows the most likely cause and possible solutions to help you fix the problem.

Symptom	Possible Causes & Solutions
1. Actual department expenses are greater than Activity Based Costs.	1. Center has idle capacity
	2. ABC costs need to be updated or process improvements identified because one or more of the following are true:
	a. Basic departmental processes, functions, or responsibilities have changed.
	b. Expenses have increased faster than volume.
	c. Volume has decreased while expenses remained the level.
	d. Labor is being loaned or utilized by other departments or areas yet the Salaries are still charged to the original department.

Symptom	*Possible Causes & Solutions*
2. Actual department expenses are less than Activity Based Costs.	1. ABC costs need to be updated because one or more of the following are true:
	a. Process improvements have been implemented which decrease the amount of resources required to perform an activity.
	b. Basic departmental processes, functions, or responsibilities have changed.
	c. Volume has increased while expenses remained level or decreased.
3. Actual labor expense is greater than Activity Based Costs.	1. Center has idle labor capacity
	2. ABC costs need to be updated or process improvements need to be identified because one or more of the following are true:
	a. Basic departmental processes, functions, or responsibilities have changed.
	b. Labor has increased faster than volume.
	c. Volume has decreased while labor has remained level.
	d. Labor is being loaned or utilized by other departments, but the Salaries are still charged to the original department.

Symptom	Possible Causes & Solutions	
4. Actual labor expense is less than Activity Based Costs.	1.	ABC costs need to be updated because one or more of the following are true:
	a.	Process improvements have been implemented which decrease the amount of labor resources required to perform an activity or function.
	b.	Basic departmental processes, functions, or responsibilities have changed.
	c.	Volume has increased while labor remained level or decreased.
5. Actual depreciation expense is greater than Activity Based Costs.	1.	ABC costs need to be updated because one or more of the following are true:
	a.	Basic departmental processes, functions, or responsibilities have changed, which decreased the services demanded in the department.
	b.	New equipment has been purchased or assigned to the department, which was not included in the original ABC costs.
	c.	Depreciation methodology has changed from straight line to double declining balance or other accelerated depreciation methodology.
	d.	Depreciable life of existing equipment has been changed or equipment has been reclassified to a category with a shorter depreciable life than was used in the original in ABC costs.

Symptom	Possible Causes & Solutions
6. Actual depreciation expense is less than Activity Based Costs.	1. ABC costs need to be updated because one or more of the following are true:
	a. Process improvements have been implemented which decrease the amount of equipment resources required to perform an activity or function.
	b. Volume has increased while depreciation expense remained level or decreased.
	c. Some of the existing equipment has become fully depreciated and has no more depreciation expense.
	d. Depreciation methodology has switched from an accelerated depreciation method to straight-line depreciation.
	e. Depreciable life of existing equipment has increased or the equipment has been reclassified to a category that has a longer depreciable life.

Symptom	Possible Causes & Solutions
7. Actual occupancy expense is greater than Activity Based Costs.	1. ABC costs need to be updated because one or more of the following are true:
	a. Basic departmental processes, functions, or responsibilities have changed, which has increased the amount of space, and utilities consumed by the department.
	b. Volume has decreased while occupancy remained level or increased.
	c. Occupancy allocation methodology has changed, increasing the amount of occupancy allocated to the department.
8. Actual occupancy expense is less than Activity Based Costs.	1. ABC costs need to be updated because one or more of the following are true:
	a. Basic departmental processes, functions, or responsibilities have changed, which has decreased the amount of space, and utilities consumed by the department.
	b. Volume has increased while occupancy remained level or decreased.
	c. Occupancy allocation methodology has changed, decreasing the amount of occupancy allocated to the department.

About the Author

William Frost has over 10 years experience in costing and process improvement, saving companies hundreds of thousands of dollars through unique approaches to profitability improvement. Frost has earned a Bachelor's in Industrial Engineering and a Master of Business Administration, in addition to other professional certifications.

978-0-595-35871-7
0-595-35871-3

www.ingramcontent.com/pod-product-compliance
Lightning Source LLC
Chambersburg PA
CBHW030943180526
45163CB00002B/687